AF593804

The Gun

The Gun

Christopher Roads

British Broadcasting Corporation

Published by the
British Broadcasting Corporation
35 Marylebone High Street
London W1M 4AA

ISBN 0 563 17208 8

First published 1978

Printed in England by Purnell & Sons Ltd.,
Paulton (Bristol) and London

Contents

Prologue

There are few more evocative subjects than that of the gun. To some the image immediately conjures to mind the winning of the West, to others the issue of law and order at home, to some again a flood of childhood memories – the first shot with a twelve bore at a pigeon on a memorable fourteenth birthday or the proud ownership of a genuine air pistol, black, shiny and undoubtedly with enough power to kill a sparrow, the envy of one's school friends. This sort of memory can confer the gun for ever with nostalgia and romance which growing older simply intensifies. To others again it stands as a reminder of the gulf between the classes or at least between the moneyed and the not so well off – can anything ever expunge the social shock of arriving at one's first shoot, an undergraduate from Oxford, with a boxlock when all about are not so discreetly enjoying their side locks? And there are those who see the gun as a mark of social superiority just as others see the horse as a great divider. But the gun lacks the bridge which television provides for the latter through showjumping. At least it was so, but one of the many objects in mind in producing a series of vignettes upon the gun for television was to rid it of the element in its mystique which works divisively.

There is enough mystery surrounding the gun to keep it always in a rather special place in technological and social history without adding to its exclusivity. Yet it is still true that the wider the gun is appreciated and the more its ownership is desired, the more its possession seems to become a mark of affluence. To far too great an extent nationally and internationally the gun is either the intriguing adjunct of the fictional criminal or the embellishment of the playboy. It's a situation made more acute through the rapid growth of television audiences and the insatiable demand for such programmes. Not only is it cheaper to churn out melodrama than worthwhile documentaries but, in our democratic age, audience ratings are a phenomenon that none dare ignore. So, the great middle ground between the gun as the instrument of the scriptwriter's villain and the gun as the plaything of the plutocrat has been ignored. It is thus the more pleasing that this opportunity has been afforded, by those who control an important part of the media, to uncover and reveal the gun in truer perspective. Fact can be more exciting than fiction.

At the present time there is a curious dichotomy. On the one hand, for the vast audiences of television melodrama there exists the amorphous pistol and nebulous submachine gun; on the other, for the growing discriminating clientele of the cinema there has been a real endeavour, over the past two decades, to get things right. It has not simply been a matter of revolvers being limited to the usual five or six shots until the hero is seen to reload, nor even of cannons at last being endowed with recoil. It is rather a matter of the operation of muzzle-loading a period arm being taken into the action, and perhaps even used ostentatiously to emphasise the authenticity of the approach.

At the same time that there is an increasing move in certain directions to a recognition of the gun as something highly specific, there is paradoxically a strong tendency towards the development of an international 'shorthand' in guns. Perhaps we owe this to Hollywood's earlier dominance of the cinema screen (and many of these productions have had a second lease of life through television), perhaps to the proliferation of the paperback. As Colt has become synonymous with the revolver, so has Winchester with the rifle. It is a little sad that national individuality is being sacrificed to what is a slowly developing mania, but mania nevertheless, to establish authenticity by staying within limits with which the public has become familiar. Certainly, if the hero of an epic about the Khyber Pass carries a Webley Fosbery automatic

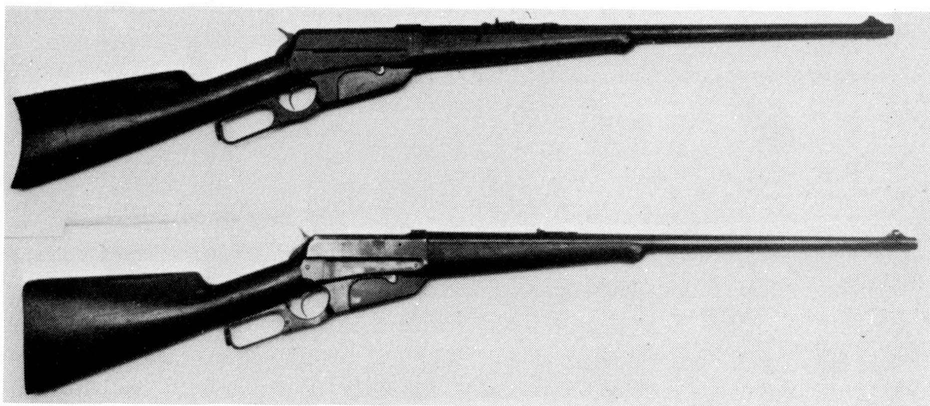

.405 Winchester Model 1895, sporting rifles. Note that one is stocked in traditional American fashion and the other in English. In fact, with the need for a powerful downward thrust on the lever the American stocking, with its positive location on the shoulder, is much superior.

revolver – as he might well have done – the very peculiarity of the arm defeats credibility. He has to be restricted to the Colt or, at the most daring, the Webley.

In spite of the forces which pull strongly towards the 'internationalisation' of the gun in fiction, there are signs that in most countries the national heritage is being recognised and enthusiastically collected. It is far cheaper, usually, to purchase arms of your own country overseas. Acquiring in Amman samples of Mausers and other early service rifles as they were adapted and carried by the Bedouin in the first decades of this century is a good way of spending at least twice and probably three times as much cash as would be needed in London for the same purchase. In some cases here you would almost be doing the vendor a service by buying off him defaced and damaged arms which no collector of Mausers or similar rifles would wish to see sullying the perfection of his representation of the factory's product. Very slowly indeed outside the bounds of one's own country recognition is growing of the folklore lure of well-used weapons. For many years yet there will be sizeable advantages in buying abroad.

There are naturally some exceptions to this rule. The obvious market, for example, for the contents of the princely armouries of India is London. So many of the magnificent sporting guns and rifles released from limbo were made by the leading English makers of the late nineteenth and early twentieth century that in many senses they formed more a part of the British than the Indian scene. Many survived their whole life in India unaltered and unadorned, others were elaborately decorated and inlaid, yet others, ravaged by insects or damaged in the field, were restocked. Today they remind us poignantly of the past glories of Imperial India and find many wealthy admirers well beyond the frontiers of the United Kingdom.

Superimposed upon this picture is the changing pattern of national wealth. Since the real growth in both the national and international interest in guns in the mid-1950s, the financial initiative in the auction room has changed hands a number of times. There was a period when the Italians seemed to buy anything, another when it was the French and then the Germans who showed their financial muscle. Now it is the turn of the Arab to take his pick. Yet in spite of all these changes London has remained pre-eminently the mart for the whole world. There was a time, not so long ago, when one of the leading auction houses would not soil its hands with modern arms, but now there is no hesitation anywhere to recognise that arms of any period are of collecting interest to someone somewhere. The pre-eminence of the English auction houses may well be seriously challenged one day, but they are aware of the need to go out to their clients as well as to maintain their London operation.

One cannot help wondering whether the ultimate threat to London, as the world's centre for art and for the purchase of arms, may not come from the derivative operations of the London houses themselves!

If fine (and not so fine) arms have taken their place alongside stocks and shares, gems and silver and many other vehicles of investment, then the main victims are those who most appreciate their ownership. Unless you can afford the price of a spare new motorcar you cannot afford to buy yourself a Borchardt automatic pistol. Unless you can go out and purchase a sea-going motor cruiser you cannot afford to own a Purdey shotgun. That is unless by the chance of inheritance you are spared the rigour of the market's valuation. Whilst it could be thought that this situation might have a very restricting effect upon the production of handbooks and manuals, this is not the case. Because so many cannot afford to acquire the genuine article they have created a very strong market for books and periodicals which convey the historical and technical story of the gun – a substitute for true ownership. The concomitant is better public access to the national and regional collections of arms – a development which has been very marked in the last twenty years.

Studying attractive illustrations, reading romantic accounts, and gazing upon actual specimens behind a solid pane of glass, constitute some sort of substitute experience, but for many it is so second-hand and remote that they look for other opportunities. If indeed they remain interested in arms they may seek to keep as close as possible to the real thing, perhaps by collecting accoutrements and accessories. Collecting bayonets is one of the most obvious avenues and has become very popular during the past fifteen years. One need not add with what effect upon price levels. Few schoolboys now could afford to collect a representative selection of bayonets. For those who can afford to indulge, however, a developing acquaintance with bayonets will lead to a desire to know as much as possible about the weapons to which they were attached.

Not every disappointed gun collector finds his consolation in bayonets. Powder flasks are very popular and so too are edged weapons. In other cases the addiction takes the form of collecting cartridges, perhaps paper case shotgun cartridges for their great variety of makers and types. The collecting of replica arms, extremely close representations of the originals, is gaining in popularity – such arms are not cheap but neither are they as costly as many of the arms from which they are copied. A surprising range of replicas is on offer in the British market alone, from muzzle-loading Enfield rifles of the mid-nineteenth century to modern semi-automatic pistols. Replicas are not resorted to solely on account of the modest prices: for many they represent the nearest to the original that the police authorities will permit them to possess.

Accessories like this nipple wrench combined with pricker, turn screw, ball drawer, mainspring cramp, etc, can easily pass unrecognised. But they are collected by many enthusiasts and much sought after.

There is a wide and legitimate field of collecting in weapon accessories. This Colt revolver powder flask of mid-19th-century manufacture is a particularly attractive item.

The subject of the law and its bearing upon the ownership and use of firearms is one upon which many books have been written and upon which there is never likely to be agreement. What is clear enough in the UK is that throughout the twentieth century the net has slowly but steadily been drawn tighter and tighter around those who are concerned with guns. Under the 1937 Firearms Act, for example, the point at which a smooth barrelled arm was classified as a firearm and therefore more stringently controlled, was when its barrel was shorter than twenty inches. It was not unreasonable for the police to argue that a really short-barrelled smooth bore gun was rather undesirable in unrestricted ownership as such arms included the notorious 'sawn-off shotgun'. Was it however so reasonable in the 1968 Firearms Act to increase the critical barrel length from twenty to twenty-four inches? We know that this was a move unwelcome to many police authorities who have to enforce the law however much it might have appeared a theoretical improvement to Home Office draughtsmen. What they seemed ignorant of was that some gunmakers (especially Churchill's) had regularly manufactured shotguns with barrels, for those who preferred lightness and manoeuvrability, which would now rank as firearms.

In America the right to bear arms is jealously guarded as one of the fundamental liberties. There is a very strong gun lobby energetically and intelligently organised by the National Rifle Association of America. Increasingly, it is being opposed by those who see through greater restriction in ownership and use of arms the path to improved public order. There has been a tendency to adduce, from the high level of homicide in which firearms are involved in the USA, a justification for further restriction upon their ownership in the United Kingdom. No argument could be more specious. There is no similarity whatsoever between the historical origins of the USA and Great Britain so far as arms are concerned. The equivalent of the American Frontier wars occurred in Britain many centuries ago – only in our empire overseas was there anything remotely approaching the situations so commonplace in late nineteenth-century America. In Britain statistics show clearly that firearms are not significantly preferred in the commission of violent crime and that violent crime is infinitely less common than it is in the States.

The form in which the law is enforced in Britain with the fundamental distinction between 'guns' and 'firearms' is reasonably sound. A firearm is any weapon which has a rifled bore to impart spin to its projectile together with those smooth bore guns with barrels shorter than twenty-four inches. In other words, generally speaking 'firearms' are arms with a fair range though, according to type, it will actually vary from a few hundred yards to over two miles. 'Guns', for which only a shotgun certificate is needed, are smooth bore arms with barrels in excess of twenty-four inches in length. By means of a shotgun certificate the authorities in a general way monitor the kind of people who are allowed possession of such arms – once a person has secured a shotgun certificate there is no restriction upon the number of such weapons he may have or on where he may use them. On the other hand he may not be allowed a shotgun certificate in the first instance unless he can show the police that he has access to suitable land, so the situation is by no means as open as it may at first seem.

For those who wish to own or use 'firearms' a firearms certificate or registered firearms dealer status is essential. The law does not recognise collector status as such. In the past few years there has been a great deal of discussion with the authorities on the possibility of collectors being recognised but there is no real evidence that we are any nearer such a move today than we were when the whole issue blew up five years ago. A firearms certificate is only granted to citizens of good character who can show that they can safely look after the weapons. This sometimes gives rise to considerable friction since so much of the judgement that is made is based upon highly subjective issues. What is safe custody for such firearms? What is reasonable usage? If you are a crofter or gillie in the Highlands of Scotland where stalking is a major occupation then you are much more likely to be able to secure a firearms certificate than if you are resident in central London and have no arrangement outside the metropolis for the use of the firearms you want.

The system has its checks and counterchecks. You require a firearms certificate to be able to own a .22 pistol for use at the local club's indoor range. Eventually you receive the certificate but only on condition that you use the pistol on authorised ranges. You may in addition have other conditions entered upon it. Their number and severity will depend entirely upon the whim of the Chief Officer of Police of the Constabulary in which you live. And there are considerable variations between one county and the next. When you wish to add to your original .22 pistol, a .303 rifle you are obliged to apply for a variation to your certificate and to satisfy the police why you require the extra weapon and, of course, that you can store it safely. So the process goes on. Each time there is a very sizeable fee to pay and each time, in most counties, a fair amount of visiting.

You will not normally be able to expand your holding of arms very far before being stiffly questioned on the justification for new arms. It is sometimes very difficult to persuade some police authorities that, even if you are a serious national or Olympic marksman, you need a different arm for each different aspect of the sport and that you may wish to shop about to find the particular make and type which fits you best. Indeed in some counties, beyond a certain point you will be allowed extra arms only if you sell some of the arms you already possess so that the total number in your possession remains the same. One thing that is also becoming increasingly clear is that membership of a shooting club is almost invariably required to justify the ownership of target or match arms. It certainly will not do to fall out with the officials at your local shooting club – if you live in a remote locality it is Hobson's choice. You need your membership to keep your arms.

Where does the collector fit into all this? For the person who goes along to the police and says that he is seriously interested in firearms or a certain branch of firearms and wishes to acquire a number of examples, the present position is extremely difficult to describe in generalisations. In some counties he will have a very difficult task in persuading the police to issue a firearms certificate or the appropriate variation. He can always appeal to the Crown Court but that is a difficult and rarely used tactic. It might be simpler to sell up and move to a county which is more accommodating! In some counties he will be able to convince the police by his membership of relevant learned societies and by his previous contributions to scholarship in the field of arms that his interest is serious and should be sustained. Clearly the field of interest must have some bearing upon the outcome. It is likely to be easier to secure a certificate for collecting obsolete nineteenth-century military rifles than modern pocket semi-automatic pistols. But though it may be more straightforward to secure permission to collect the former, it is likely to bring him closer to the most shadowy area of all – that of 'antique' firearms.

What is an 'antique' firearm? The answer very much depends upon whom you ask and where you ask it. For Customs and Excise officers it tends to be any arm over one hundred years old. For some police authorities it is limited to muzzle-loaders. A Colt Navy .36 muzzle-loading revolver made in 1855 is unquestionably an antique. A replica of the same revolver made in Italy in about 1965 can be so exact in appearance that it is virtually indistinguishable from the original. Woe betide you if you cannot recognise it for what it is, for as a modern copy it is a 'firearm' and you need a firearms certificate properly varied to cover it. If you show your genuine Colt Navy muzzle-loading revolver proudly to your friend and he decides to see how it works and fires it, he has immediately broken the law. It has become a 'firearm' and with this use it ceases to be an 'antique'. One consequence of this position is that at the moment of sale your revolver, through being used, is a 'firearm' on your certificate but, if the vendor regards it only as an 'antique', having himself no intention of using it, the arm then vanishes from police records.

In the middle decades of the nineteenth century a great variety of different

Pin-fire drawn-brass revolver cartridges.

breech-loading systems were tried. One of the most widely manufactured was the needle rifle. It employed a papiermâché cartridge with the percussion element inside it. Ignition therefore could be effected only when a needle had penetrated the cardboard and struck the pellet. Such arms are now regarded by most police forces as antiques. Probably nearly as many constabularies regard all breech-loading systems which used cartridges without the incorporation of ignition, such as the capping breechloaders, as antiques too. Those breech-loaders, and there were not many of them, which used metallic cartridges not incorporating a cap or other percussion element are almost equally widely regarded as antiques. These and indeed all the early breechloaders are comparatively scarce and sometimes quite rare, usually commanding fairly high sums in the auction rooms. Moreover, if you know enough about firearms to be able successfully to improvise ammunition for them, then you could rather more easily improvise a modern arm from commonly available industrial components.

The difficulty in the definition of antique arms begins to arise with the pinfire system. Pinfire ammunition was made until well into this century but speaking generally pinfire arms have been superseded for about a hundred years. As a system the pinfire had its critics but for low-powered revolvers, and some other applications, arms survive to this day in fair quantities. Certainly they often have a Victorian look about them, and as such there are many who collect them. But are they 'antiques'? The theoretical answer is probably 'no', if individually they can be shown to have been made less than one hundred years ago. Practically speaking, in some constabularies in Britain, pinfires are regarded as antiques but in most they are not. What is not clear is whether any distinction is made between those older and those younger than one hundred years old.

If there are constabularies accepting pinfires as antiques, then the very rare teat-fire cartridge breechloader (which was one with the percussion composition in a teat-like extension, at the rear of the brass cartridge case) and the fairly rare large-calibre, rimfire breechloaders ought equally to be regarded as antiques. There has probably not been a test case in the courts to decide this point but, given that the dates of manufacture were more than one hundred years ago, it is very likely that the courts would sustain the view that such breechloaders are antiques.

No student of British military firearms will be around very long before he encounters the very large calibre, centre-fire rifles manufactured over one hundred years ago. Perhaps the most common is the .577 Snider. These have generally been regarded as 'firearms' and not as antiques (though they may have been manufactured as early as 1864) because ammunition for them has not been out of production long enough for it to be practically unprocurable. On the other hand occasional centre-fire breechloaders turn up with a high rarity value, manufactured at any date between 1859 and 1876, but chambered for experimental or private cartridges which are today entirely unobtainable. Some are so rare that examples of the cartridges cannot be found in any of the reference collections. Is it not reasonable to regard such arms as antiques? In America they would be, but no one has yet tried the law in this country. So if you wish to collect in this area you will need a firearms certificate with appropriate variations, but there should be little difficulty in obtaining them, given *bona fides,* in most constabularies.

As the law stands at present, if you were to decide to form a collection of short sections of rifled barrels, to show the great variety of rifling types and calibres, you would not be able to do so unless you had obtained a firearms certificate. Any component of a firearm is treated as if it were a firearm so there is no facile field for collecting in this direction. You would be better advised to collect smooth-bored rifles. As a weapon with a smooth-bored barrel more than twenty-four inches long is not a firearm, some years ago it occurred to a number of dealers that they might take surplus British military rifles, such as the SMLE and the Enfield No 4, and bore the barrels out so that the rifling was entirely removed. Outwardly the arm remains exactly as it was but in the eyes of the law it has become a shotgun. They are not cheap to collect but, subject to the possession of a shotgun certificate, they can be collected and are

William Ellis Metford, perhaps the most talented and influential of all British rifle designers of the 19th century.

Waiting for duck with a 60-inch barrelled 8-bore of about 1760 vintage is pretty fatiguing unless the gun is held at the high port, not so much in hope of flying quarry but rather the sitting bird.

The Martini-Henry did not get its reputation for kicking like a mule without real justification.

becoming in some quarters a not unpopular alternative. Whilst the rifles which are so modified are common, no museum is likely to complain, but if, through a tightening of the law in other directions, the habit were to begin to embrace rarer arms, then many people would bitterly deplore the consequent erosion of our heritage. It is in fact generally accepted in Britain today that arms are a part of our heritage and that 'deactivisation' is a practice which should not be permitted. Fortunately, the law gives no advantage whatsoever to 'deactivating' an arm (save in the special case of the smooth-bored 'rifle'), so there should be nothing to worry about.

The other side of this coin does have a slightly bizarre appearance. Because no form of deactivisation is recognised by law, when, for example, a crashed aircraft is exhumed by enthusiasts in an aircraft preservation society, they will usually find that they are not permitted, without the issue of a firearms certificate, to keep any of the firearms on board even though they may be no more than corroded lumps of metal and utterly unserviceable. Usually in fact they will be machine guns and as such are prohibited weapons so the dilemma of the finders and the authorities could seem to be the more intense. Actually all such arms are deemed to be the property of the Crown and the Ministry of Defence is held responsible for them.

Another pitfall that should be taken into account by those who console themselves collecting smooth-bored rifles is the situation regarding oval-bore rifles. To the uninitiated an oval-bore rifle, with only a few thousandths of an inch difference between the major and minor axis of the rifling, looks as if it is a smooth-bore arm. In fact the oval-bore system works as well as one depending on obvious grooves and is quite often found in sporting rifles. Pistols with oval- or elliptical-bore rifling will be rated as firearms on account of their barrel lengths. Thus, oval bores must be ranked as 'firearms' and treated with all the formality which that implies.

If it seems that over the definition of an 'antique' firearm the law is in urgent need of revision, then the point has been missed. The great variety of systems, the many variations upon nearly every theme, conspire to make it almost impossible to draft a neat and practical definition of an 'antique' firearm. Many have tried to do so but no one has managed to produce a definition that appeals to most of the parties involved and is practical. It is no use devising a system that requires a degree in engineering to understand it. Whatever is laid down has to be applied all over the country by police and layman alike with no engineering or historical training, which makes an improved definition of an antique firearm a challenge indeed.

For those who may be deterred from collecting in the central field of guns and firearms there is no easy alternative in the direction of ammunition.

Anyone who has examined the base of a metallic cartridge with its legend of essential information will have been struck by a superficial resemblance to numismatic items. This similarity is found especially in the area of military cartridge cases, with their type and calibre designations, their arsenal marks, dates, and quite frequently different coloured annuli around the cap. Many people do collect them, but for all cartridges intended for firearms they first have to obtain a firearms certificate and then have to ensure the necessary variations are recorded. It is an elaborate and tedious business and is perhaps one of the principal reasons why the number of collectors is still relatively small.

By the time you have read this book you should see arms in a somewhat wider context than a coin collector views his pieces or a stamp collector his acquisitions. Indeed you should have decided – if you are ever moved to collect – which area commands your greatest interest. Where one collects is nearly always a compromise between interest, pocket and legal restraints. But wherever you decide to settle, the question which immediately arises is how to go about it.

You will want to know where to acquire relevant arms and you will want to know how to find out as much as possible about your chosen field. In arms, scholarship is advancing at a rapid pace. Keeping abreast of the newest discoveries, absorbing the newest theories can be done either by joining the appropriate society or subscribing to the relevant journals or preferably doing both. Curiously, though rising prices have forced many scholar-collectors to abandon their favourite fields, the strong stimulus from investment collecting for good clear guide books to every sub-field has greatly contributed to a far wider range of publications than there was available only a few years ago. It is only when one examines a recent catalogue of available books from one of the firms specialising in this area that one realises how vast a subject 'the gun' is and how numerous are its sub-fields.

There is no better place to acquire specimens for your collection (or even to adorn your house if they are antiques and not subject to legal requirements of safe custody) than the auction room. Every year the opportunities for acquisition by private purchase seem to diminish. Only twenty years ago there were still exciting chances of picking up very desirable antique arms in country house sales. Now, if any appear, it is more likely that they will be sold well over the London auction-room price level than given away below it. The only exception to this that I have recently observed is where an arm in a country sale is somewhat obscure and actually very rare. It is surprising how often those in the auction room, vendors and would-be purchasers alike, fail to identify an arm which is slightly out of the normal pattern. A few years back

Coiled-brass, drawn-copper and drawn-brass cartridge cases (L to R).

one of the leading auctioneers in London offered for sale, unidentified for what it actually was, one of the rarest of all British military pistols, and the same auctioneers also sold the rarest of all nineteenth-century British military rifles, identified as being a different and only scarce type. Similarly it was another leading British auctioneer who sold unrecognised perhaps the rarest variation of the British Minié rifle of 1851, when the difference was as obvious as three grooves in the rifling instead of the usual four!

If there is a lesson to be learnt from a long acquaintance with arms it is that even leading experts can make mistakes and can overlook the obvious. The best advice that anyone new to the field can be given is: first, choose your speciality, then study it closely from the best available books and the examples available in public collections, and, so equipped, scour the auction rooms. Never trust anyone else's identification; always make your own.

The auction room is the best place to acquire guns even in these days of the purchaser having to pay a commission for the privilege of buying. Try, however, not to rely on the auctioneers for their statements on condition. As with almost every branch of collecting, condition is all-important. A common gun in very fine condition is almost invariably worth more than a rare gun in a poor state. The trouble with condition is that it is subjective. Unless an arm is described as being in new condition there must be a doubt. Most collectors try to acquire arms with as much original finish as possible. Few want arms where, though only twenty per cent of the original finish is missing, it is missing from the highlights. The term 'sleeper' has crept into auctioneers' jargon which is useful but does not eliminate the high degree of subjectivity inherent in any verbal description. And as collectors and shooters are usually different animals, a shooter in the auction room is well advised to study carefully the condition of the bore and bore closure.

No arm may be sold at auction if it is not in proof and it can go out of proof very easily if wear opens up tolerances. Nevertheless the rifling can become very eroded and an arm become hopeless for shooting without it going out of proof – so buyer beware! With many older arms the special cartridges necessary for proof firing are themselves unobtainable, so the arm will be issued by the proof house with a certificate of exemption from proof. In other words the arm may be kept as a curio or antique but it is not to be shot. Not infrequently the collector can do quite well at an auction by buying arms which have failed proof. Legally they cannot then be sold as arms so they are sold under the formula 'the major parts of . . .' Usually this does not mean a burst barrel and when assembled the arm may look quite perfect to the lay eye. It would be useless to the shooter, but, perhaps, an ideal acquisition for the collector.

There is only one way to know what to acquire and that is to acquire a number of items that one does not want. This does not mean that one falls out of love with one's own poor specimen for envy of the finer example belonging to a friend, though this can happen, but rather that arms which have been refinished can pass muster in some conditions but stand revealed as impostors when the light changes. Probably, not more than one in a dozen refinished arms has gained anything in the process. Indeed, if refinishing can be detected it is not worth doing. There are those who will pay a premium for a refinished arm compared with one left in its 'natural' state. Usually it is the reverse since refinishing so often means that sharp edges are blurred, that inscriptions are dulled, that straight lines become undulating, that browning becomes blueing, that age toning yields to cheaper brilliance and that close fits become sloppy junctions. The moral of the story is 'if in doubt don't'. Refinishing is usually an expensive and disappointing waste of time.

Whilst refinishing is anathema, professional restoration is another matter. So too is 'in service' repair. Quite often arms appear which show considerable splicing of walnut inserts. On the whole these are safe being the product of professional repairs in the active life of the arm. Arms were broken or damaged in service and were either repaired in the field or by the government establishment set up for the purpose. Nevertheless, always look carefully at splicings: they can be proof of unauthorised alterations of a common arm to make it seem a rarer pattern. They can even be part of the evidence pointing to a reconversion back to an original pattern or type. The classic example of this is the conversion back to flintlock of locks which, whilst in original use, were converted from flintlock to percussion. There is good business sense in the reconversion since flintlocks are almost always worth much more than percussion locks. There may too be strong aesthetic justification but the reconverted arm is still only reconverted!

Long before anyone new to the field has been able to put into practice half the advice tendered in these paragraphs, he will feel a need to swap experiences, to discuss mounting theories and indeed generally to contribute to the gradual process of historical research into arms development. Arms research, like most other fields, is a painstaking business of the investigation of written and photographic sources and then correlation with such arms as have survived. At times either the arm alone survives defying anyone to place it in context or the record is discovered proving, sometimes from a photograph, that a particular arm was made though no example can be found. For those whose interests lie essentially in the earlier period, in general terms before about 1860, the obvious society to join is the Arms and Armour Society, but for those whose real interest starts about 1865 the relevant learned society is the Historical Breechloading Small Arms Association (the HBSA) which is based at the Imperial War Museum in Lambeth Road, London SE1. Both societies welcome all classes of members: student, associate or full. Both publish journals and have lectures: the HBSA has monthly meetings and lectures on the third Monday of each month.

The collector is less well served than the shooter or marksman. The marksman simply has to join his nearest club, and he can almost automatically procure a firearms certificate from the police. Betwixt and between there are those who are both. They may, of course, indulge separately in each field or they may merge their interests. The HBSA actually has a shooting section and holds occasional shoots especially for historical firearms. The Vintage Arms Association exists exclusively for the firing of older arms, though there is not quite so much variety as the name implies. In the firing of arms which may be as much as a hundred years old the first consideration is safety. This essentially means that only arms in good condition and loaded strictly in accordance with the original ammunition specification are permitted. Achieving this is not quite as easy as it sounds. In some cases the original type of powder has long since ceased to be manufactured which means that a modern equivalent has to be found, not always a straightforward task.

There is no better way of appreciating the real qualities of the arms that our forebears carried and used than to carry and use them ourselves. It is only in this way that we really understand why some designs survived and others were rapidly ditched. It also brings home the tactical limitations that went with different systems. The Martini-Henry's difficult extraction, the Money and Walker's clumsiness of breech operation, the general facility of the Snider in spite of the need to pick the fired cartridge out of the shoe or to eject it by inverting the whole weapon, the hand lacerating tendencies of the Mauser 7.62 mm broomhandle pistol, the viciously painful recoil characteristic of the Bland single trigger 20 bore pistol, the stinging escape of gas at the breech of the Sharps carbine, the laughable lack of power in the Sea Service muzzle-loading pistol, the almost equal futility of the .320 pocket revolver, the lead spitting habits of the Smith and Wesson .38 revolver – all these and countless other foibles can still be experienced, and with that experience will dawn an infinitely clearer comprehension of how one development followed another and why some arms though technically dazzling were dead ends in the evolutionary progress.

First find your weapon then ensure its safety. Next establish to what extent it is likely to perform typically of its type. It is not fair to judge the accuracy of a particular arm by its performance today, especially if you have access to only one example and that is worn. It needs only a slight warping of the fore end to make a nonsense of such a trial or a somewhat bell mouthed muzzle (quite a common occurrence through hard use and much cleaning) which will entirely spoil the accuracy of fire. In addition to the arm's immediate vulnerability is the shortfall in the ammunition. If you are fortunate enough to possess original ammunition and have justified to yourself its use (when others might regard it in its own right as antique and to be cherished not disposed of), then the probability is that it will perform only at a very low level of efficiency. Caps in particular are liable to heavy deterioration. It is a well-known fact that weak ignition is the death of accuracy since it inevitably means irregular ignition of the charge. And if you manufacture your own ammunition to meet this challenge do not imagine it is easy to duplicate the powder.

The majority of historical rifles and pistols likely to be fired today are proved for black powder. The manufacture of black powder in Great Britain ceased finally, so we are told, in 1976. For many years the product of the mills had been very inferior to that produced in the nineteenth century. Then, it was recognised that the type and manufacture of the charcoal was all important. The result is that modern black powder is usually very much less powerful than its antecedents. In somewhat comparable form some of the early smokeless powders were relatively unstable and have long since passed their prime. If anyone wants to test the vulnerability of powders to storage conditions and to see how the powder can vary for any one batch of ammunition over fifty years, let him select the most accurate batch of rifle ammunition he can find and then store it for four months at a temperature of 100°F – not an unreasonable one compared with tropical levels. If at the end of the period the ammunition is test fired it will be found to have declined sharply in consistency. That is a consequence solely of heat, and the combination of heat and humidity is even more destructive.

For all these cautions, limitations and reservations, there is no substitute for trying the arms oneself. And yet how can all those, or even one in a hundred of those who would like to, actually do so? There are still rifles and pistols to be bought, there are even those to be found in the auction room cased with their original ammunition and sometimes in good condition; more rarely still there are some with all the reloading equipment cased with them. So, for a few the opportunities afforded by the HBSA and the Vintage Arms Association will continue to be grasped. For the rest of us there is perhaps one substitute: a genuine and exact film record of what happens when these obsolete arms are fired. A film record which shows both the functioning of the loading and breech mechanisms and the recoil characteristics. That is what we have tried to achieve in the television series made with BBC Chronicle. In the space of ten short programmes each only fifteen minutes long, one can only sample here and there the vast legion of arms that has emanated from so many parts of the world over the past five hundred years.

The film series is obviously much more than a straight record of the performance of selected individual weapons. It is an attempt to tell the story of the development of the gun, setting within their historical context a selection of arms which represent an amalgam of those which are milestones in the evolution of the gun with those which are typical and likely to be encountered today. There is nothing like the prospect of private ownership to heighten interest, so there is little sense in not anchoring the saga to everyday experience. What we were able to do in the course of making the series was to operate and fire many more arms than actually appeared in the final version, in effect to begin to establish an audiovisual data bank on the gun. It is a project which should be continued – the creation of visual bricks, as it were – which one day may be used in another structure illuminating perhaps other aspects of the total theme. One can take as an analogy the battleship: there is no surviving example of a British battleship or of a Second World War warship demonstrating its speed and its fire power. To comprehend these giants of technology, we have to rely solely upon the written word and the visual record. Only a film record conveys the performance really effectively. This must be increasingly true for the gun itself and especially for the rarer and earlier forms of firearm.

1

The Great Leveller

The classic form of the gun, a metal tube or barrel from which a round or spherical projectile is shot by means of a charge mainly consumed in the barrel, is fast becoming one of the worked-out ideas of the past. At least that is the position with artillery, although with small arms the reverse is probably true. Inventions since the Second World War – such as the Gyrojet, which depends on the rocket action of a small arms projectile – existed briefly only as curiosities and are now themselves historic. In the field of small arms the preoccupation of the age is with reducing weight and especially the weight of ammunition carried. One way of achieving this, as well as a major simplification of design, is by the abolition of the brass cartridge case. In a curious way this change, which is not likely to be seen widely yet, looks back to the era of muzzle-loading arms with their simple use of propellant and projectile.

At present the trend in military small arms is almost universally to small calibres – to bore sizes even below 5 mm. Tendencies in small arms in the late twentieth century contrast sharply with ordnance trends in the early part of this century. Then it seemed as if guns simply went on getting bigger. Such giants as the 15″ and 16″ really had to be mounted in ships, otherwise they were exceedingly inflexible to use. For a time they secured the British Empire as certainly as intercontinental ballistic missiles defend American hegemony today, or vast siege engines depending on counterweights or tension once helped cement the might of the Roman Empire. With the 15″ gun even the Straits of Dover shrank to the status of a ditch, just as, with a catapult, man could keep a river between him and his adversary.

For most of recorded history man has found a special attraction in avoiding the direct test of physical strength. Massive siege engines and humble slings alike gave him that satisfying ability of striking from afar. With siege engines he might pay a high price in physical exertion, loading and firing, but he

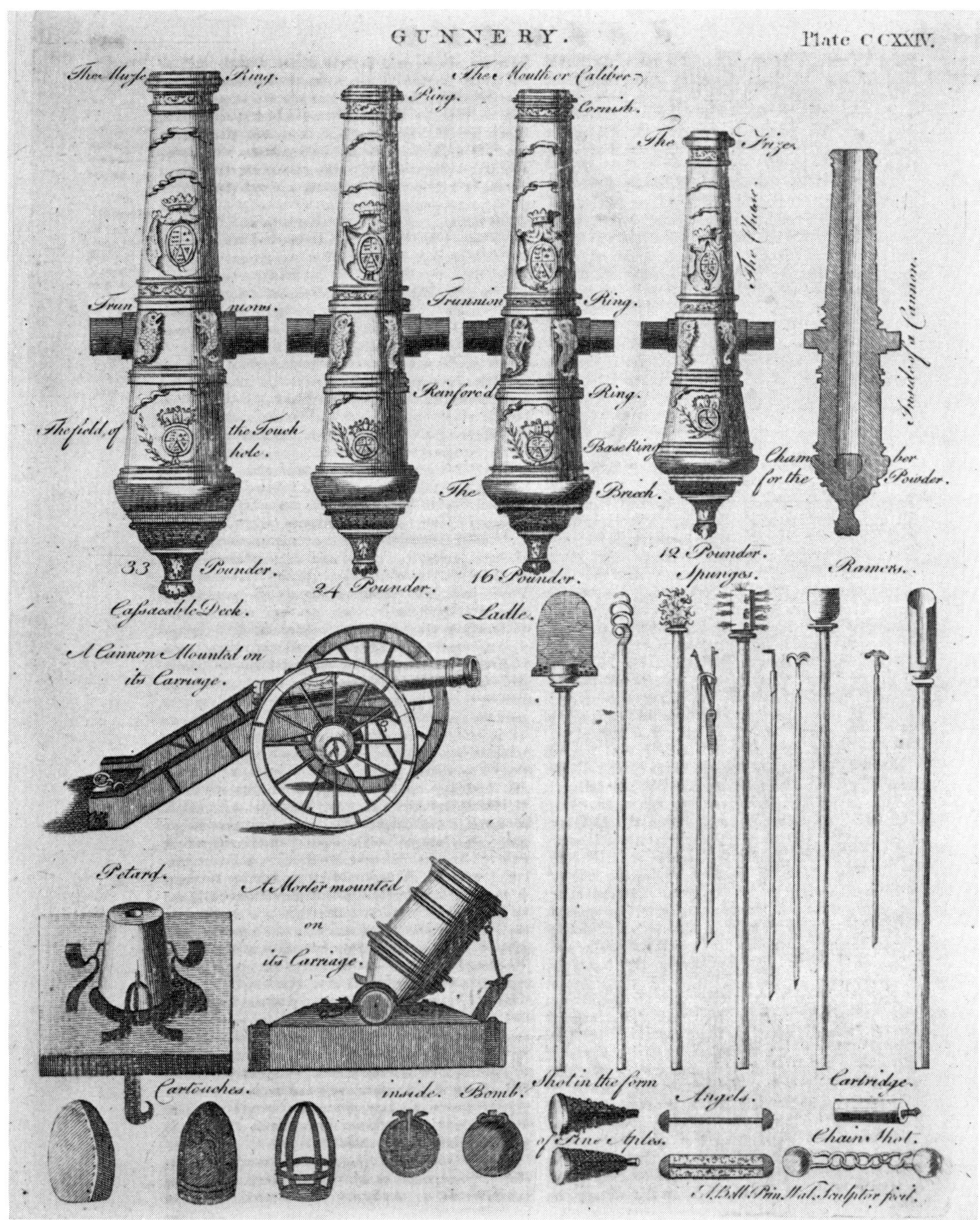

Guns and ramrods.

avoided the direct test of personal skill. In one sense, behind such an engine the humblest peasant in the land was the equal of any man. The French nobility found their rank no protection from peasant arrows at Agincourt and the Scots were in a similar position at Flodden field. Whilst in our own times we know that neither dukes nor presidents can deny the assassin who strikes from a distance.

Before the discovery of gunpowder – energy locked into a portable and readily releasable form – the best possible use was made of tensioning elastic media or releasing counterweights. Both were processes which took time as well as sweat. So too did bringing these engines to bear on the enemy. Moving them, even when dismantled, must have been a nightmare, bearing in mind the state of the roads. In such warfare, even in classical times, we know that total reliance was by no means placed on engines of these types. When there was a man of genius on hand, such as Archimedes at the siege of Syracuse, fire could be added to the orthodox armoury of warfare. The famous Greek fire was made either through the use of burning glasses or mirrors, or a true incendiary composition. To what extent Greek fire was used in a self-projecting fashion has yet to be established by historians. It is tempting to see it as the natural forerunner of gunpowder, but we know that Greek fire was normally projected by orthodox siege engines.

Gunpowder offered a considerable advantage to the artillerist whose impedimenta, whilst extensive, were greatly reduced in comparison with his predecessors'. However, the converse was the case in the field of small arms – no early hand gun could be compared with the bow in terms of military efficiency. The long bow and the cross bow were accurate, had relatively high penetrative power and were fast to fire. All they lacked was the 'thunder and lightning' effect. Once that counted for less – and there is nothing like familiarity for breeding contempt – the bow was seen to be much more ruthlessly efficient. It cannot be argued that the ordinary musket available to the common soldier bore any military comparison with the bow until the eighteenth century. Sadly, it needed much less time to train a musketeer to a passable standard than it did a bowman. Or to put it another and very familiar way, in a relatively sophisticated society no one concerned with the economics of a situation uses a highly skilled man and a simple machine when he is offered an unskilled man and a complex machine, assuming of course that the machine is not too costly.

The origins of gunpowder will probably never be generally agreed. An incendiary composition was known to the Indians and to the Chinese around the year AD 100 but it never seems to have been used for propellant purposes. In spite of all that might be inferred from the long history of Chinese experimentation in the general field of powders, it was actually in Europe that true gunpowder was first described. However, the basic information from which the discovery was made undoubtedly came from China via the Arabs to Europe. There is, for example, an Arab treatise written before 1248 by Ibn al Baytar which shows that the author was well acquainted with saltpetre, called the snow of China ('thaljal-Sin'). Claims have been made for the invention of gunpowder by, or on behalf of, a number of different people. Traditionally, Berthold Schwartz, or the Black Monk, was accredited the honour of the invention but it was more likely Albertus Magnus's. Arguing the pros and cons of the identity of the actual inventor on present available evidence is likely to be rather unproductive: all we do know certainly is that the invention was announced to Europe in about 1250 by the English scholar, Roger Bacon, in his *Liber Ignium (Book of Fires).* Indeed 'announced' is the only fair description. In his *Opus Tertium* Bacon wrote: 'By the flash and combustion of fires, and by the horror of sounds, wonders can be wrought, and at any distance that we wish so that a man can hardly protect himself or endure it.'

The invention of gunpowder ranks with the inventions of the wheel and printing as one of those moments when mankind took a giant step forward in his uneasy progress towards our modern state of technological sophistication. Like those two other great inventions it could be used for good or ill, as the war chariot, the armoured car or the propaganda leaflet remind us.

Making gunpowder was an art and science. Made without precision it could be so slow burning that it would scarcely merit the description of rocket powder, or so variable that the consequences of its use were quite unpredictable. The basic element was charcoal which cannot simply be made from any wood. Only a very limited number of timbers are acceptable – alder, dogwood or beech are most commonly used. The charcoal has to be prepared with great care to retain its necessary qualities: the temperature of carbonising of the charcoal is critical to performance. In this direction the technique has changed very little down the ages. It is a pity that after all these centuries the manufacture of gunpowder finally ceased in Great Britain in 1976.

As with the manufacture of charcoal so with that of gunpowder itself – traditional methods have changed very little. The original formula in the *Liber Ignium* was contained in an elaborate anagram which has been interpreted as seven parts of saltpetre to five parts each of charcoal and sulphur. By 1350, a century after Bacon's book, English gunpowder was given as six parts saltpetre to two of charcoal and one of sulphur, but it is a mistake to attach too much significance to the precise ratio of the components. Much more important were the problems of making gunpowder easier to transport and less susceptible to water.

A significant innovation was making the components wet so that their incorporation was complete. This method also greatly reduced the danger of an explosion. The components were so integrated that they could not separate out of their amalgamation when shaken and jolted as they were transported. Finally, each grain of powder could be glazed so that it was much less prone to taking up moisture.

Gunpowder arrived on the European stage in 1250; yet there seems to be no evidence for an earlier dating of any gun than about the third decade of the fourteenth century. One of the earliest references to cannon in English sources seems to be in the manuscript 'De Officiis Regium' which was dedicated to Edward III and dated 1326. What is there illustrated is a large vase or pot from which is being shot an arrowlike projectile. It is fascinating that this, perhaps one of the earliest illustrations of a gun, depicts the use of this type of projectile – so much in arms developments seems to run in cycles and this is no exception. Today amongst the most sophisticated of modern projectiles for the soldier are compound flechette – arrow – missiles. There is a literary reference to what might be bearers of portable firearms in an Italian document of about 1281. But there is no clue as to who actually invented the gun. The identity of man's greatest benefactor will probably remain a secret for ever.

The oldest known hand cannon is in Sweden and dates from about 1350, but it is only a small version of a full-size cannon. With contemporary powder of low power a cannon had to have a reasonably large size to be at all effective. Thus there were few on the battlefield of Crécy in 1346 but there were many at the siege of Calais immediately afterwards. On the battlefield, whilst gunners served their cannon, the arm which really held sway was the bow, and for a long time the soldier was never more effective individually than when trained to carry and use one. The portability of the bow was one of its major attractions, contrasting very sharply with the cumbersome character of larger cannon. The largest ordnance were in fact often breechloaders, and this considerably simplified both loading and land transportation.

The oldest hand cannon of English origin comes from Castle Rising and dates from the fifteenth century. It is of the simplest possible construction of traditional barrel form – two pieces of metal were formed around a mandrel, welded and then held together by hoops, which were placed in position red hot so that as they cooled and shrank they held the barrel together. Light though this construction might seem, it was still sufficiently strong to withstand the explosion of the charge which was simply touched off with a burning match. The gun was roughly pointed by the rearwards extension to the barrel: as yet, this was completely devoid of any butt-like form.

It is not very rewarding to try to adduce patterns in the development of the form of the hand gun where none existed. The only common feature was that the barrel sat more or less within a wooden surround, which in its rearwards extension anticipated the role of the more modern stock, sometimes a wooden stock or tiller fitted into a socket which itself was formed integrally with the chamber end of the barrel. If the former can be seen by the over-imaginative as the prototype of the normal modern stock, then the latter could be regarded, even more figuratively, as the forerunner of the divided military stock which slowly appears from about 1870.

Loading a gun was a simple operation – the powder was poured down the barrel, then wadding was rammed in position over it to confine it. Lastly a ball or suitable projectile was loaded and, where necessary, this was retained in position by an over-wad. A small quantity of fine powder was placed in the touch hole and ignited with a burning match applied by hand. As the touch hole connected directly with the powder in the barrel, the main charge ignited almost, but not quite, simultaneously: however simple an operation, it still took time. There was no chance at all of firing a quick second shot: moreover, the business of keeping a burning match constantly available called for considerable ingenuity.

Inevitably the two goals, which became evident early in the gun's development, were first, achieving a capacity to fire more than one shot, so that there was something in reserve after the first discharge, and secondly, to find a mechanical means of holding and placing the burning match in the priming powder.

The simplest way of achieving multishot capacity was to increase the number of barrels and soon this was quite widely found. Another method involved loading the charges one after the other in the same barrel, and then firing them in succession from the muzzle backwards. By the seventeenth century, magazine-loading the separate components, so that they came together in fireable form in the chamber of the gun, could be procured – but at a price.

The second goal, of mechanising the application of the match to the powder, was achieved some time in the fifteenth century. Like so many of the important steps in the evolution of the gun it was the product of an unknown inventor. Possibly it was the idea of more than one designer and was conceived in different parts of Europe more or less contemporaneously. But to what extent it evolved directly from the mechanism of a crossbow can only be guessed.

The mechanism which applied the match was called the matchlock. It consisted simply of a pivoted arm or serpentine, which held the match, usually clamped, so shaped and positioned that when the firer saw the right

With all early guns using match or flint ignition, the existence of an open vent through which the charge was fired allowed violent escape of gas at the breech, often to the danger of the firer.

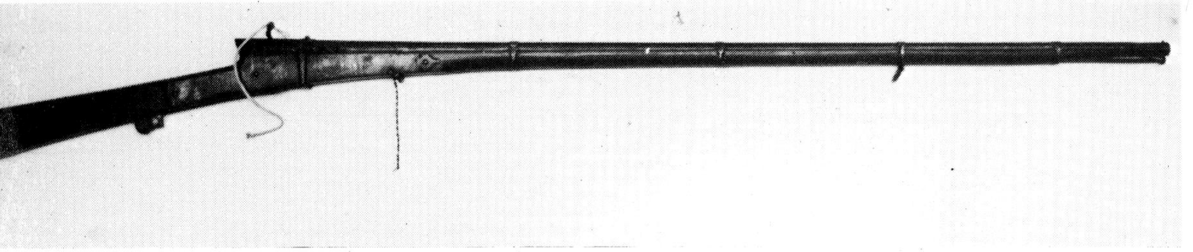

Matchlock weapons died out in Europe in the 18th century but in India and other parts of Asia they were made and used well into the 19th century. This is a typical arm of Sind manufacture.

aim and pressed the trigger or connecting rod the match descended into the priming powder. In most of the early European matchlocks, the match moves towards the eye, being pivoted beyond the pan; but in the Sind types of the late eighteenth and early nineteenth centuries which are commonly encountered today, the serpentine moves away from the eye.

The existence of a matchlock was a great stimulus to the lightening and refining of the hand gun. Slowly, as the sixteenth century wore on, the matchlock became an aesthetically attractive possession and its functioning relatively trouble free. With improving mechanical efficiency naturally went widening military employment. Nevertheless it was not until 1525 that it was credited with a significant success on the battlefield, when the French king, Francis I, was captured as a result of its effective use in enfilade fire.

There is always room for improvement, and the matchlock was no exception to the rule. By the late fifteenth century it had certainly become a sophisticated and elegant arm. By then the pan was usually covered so that the powder was better protected from the weather; often a fence to the rear of the pan shielded the firer's eye from flying grains of burning powder; and the back sight was sometimes quite elaborate, allowing a really scientific attempt to match elevation to distance. But for all this refinement the arm was still very vulnerable in bad weather. What was needed next was a self-igniting lock.

Dresden's famous Monk's Gun, invented by an unknown German in about 1475, should have ushered in a new era. For the first time there was no need to tend a burning match. Amazingly the Monk's Gun remained unique, uncopied. Perhaps, on second thoughts, this is not so amazing in the context of the fate of most of the original inventions in the development of the gun.

The invention of the self-igniting lock, which actually did usher in the new era, occurred around the year 1500, so there was not a long pause. It took the form of a wheel-lock, where the rapid revolution of a wheel against a block of pyrites struck out a shower of sparks which directly ignited the priming

Firing a replica of the remarkable late-15th-century Monk's Gun – the first-known self-igniting lock.

7.62-mm British Army self-loading rifle with its Rank night sight is a highly specialised and expensive piece of equipment.

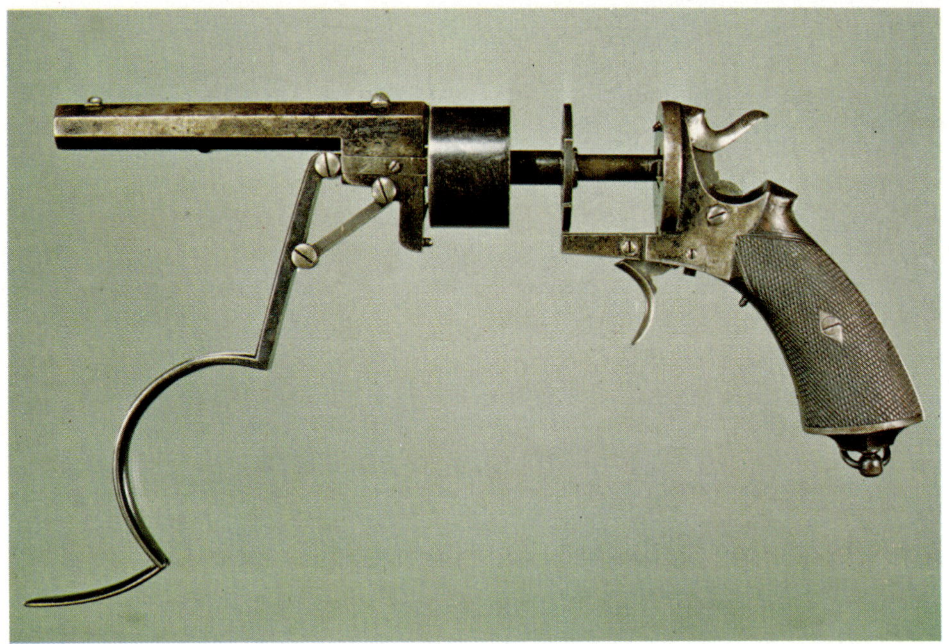

The Galand's is generally typical of the many ingenious mechanisms which, in the 1870s and 1880s, were devised to effect the simultaneous ejection of all fired cartridge cases from the chamber of a revolver.

An Historical Breech-loading Small Arms Association range practice with early breech-loading pistols and revolver.

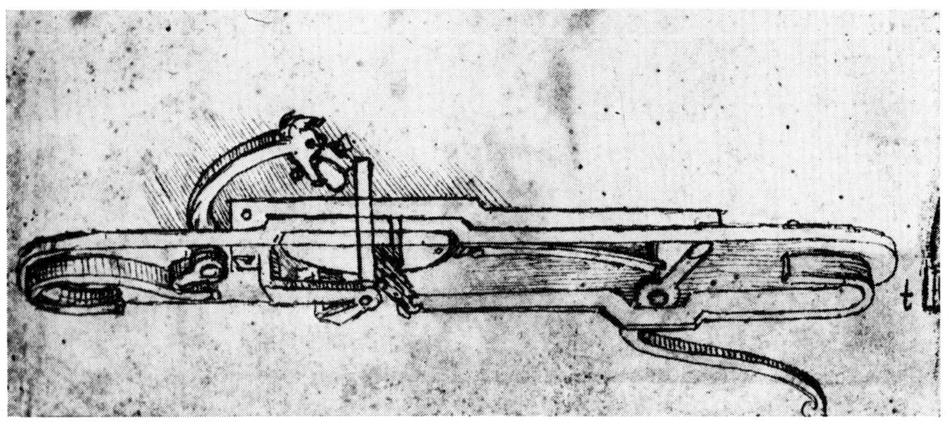

Leonardo da Vinci's famous sketches of a wheel-lock seem to be of a practical design, but whether of his genius or another's is not easily established.

powder. Once again there is a mystery over the actual inventor. The man most commonly ascribed the honour is Leonardo da Vinci, who certainly sketched a form of wheel-lock which works, but whether he was sketching an idea already current or one of his own remains still to be resolved. That the sketch in the *Codex Atlanticus* can be converted into a working model does not really help to solve the mystery.

The wheel-lock had a very certain operation since the top edge of the wheel, where the sparks were generated, was actually enclosed in the priming pan which was covered until automatically uncovered at the instant of firing. What is also apparent about this lock, however, is that it must have been expensive – too expensive ever to become part of the arm of the common soldier. It was more vulnerable to harsh treatment than the matchlock. Moreover, if the firer lost the spanner or key which wound the mainspring, then he was out of action until a new one could be filed up by an armourer.

How often was a wheel-lock fired with a match because the mechanism had broken or jammed? The mechanism was comparatively delicate and certainly not suitable for cost-cutting cheap manufacture. Nonetheless it seems that the wheel-lock was a well-advanced mechanism only eighty years after Leonardo's drawing was executed in the *Codex Atlanticus.* Well into the seventeenth century the wealthy and a few select troops enjoyed the advantages of the self-igniting wheel-lock, applied to both the gun and pistol, while the armies of Europe carried and fought with the matchlock musket and carbine. It was not until the emergence of the snap haunce and the flintlock that the common soldier began to enjoy the advantages of a self-igniting lock.

2
Ars Gratia Artis

So fine are the guns made for royalty and the aristocracy that the point can be reached when adornment and embellishment seriously erode practicality and efficiency. In some cases it was definitely *ars gratia artis* – art for the sake of art – but whatever the degree of ornamentation they were all still lethal weapons. Although fashions change and some mechanisms lend themselves more to elaborate treatment than others, there are basically two approaches to the creation of the finest arms: one is ostentatious, the other is the soul of discretion. *Ars est celare artem* might well be the motto of today's leading English gunmakers or the Regency makers, contrasted with those who worked for the seventeenth- and eighteenth-century French court.

Inverted snobbery is a subtle monster. Those who proudly own a Boss, or Purdey, or Holland & Holland, have no right to despise those who made and used arms of great artistic elaboration. For much longer periods in history those who can afford it have elected to make the fact strikingly apparent in their sporting arms rather than to conceal it to all but the initiated.

A fine musket of the seventeenth century gave endless scope not simply to lock-maker and barrel-maker but also to the stock-maker. He was given a marvellous opportunity for using his fertile imagination in a torrent of brilliantly conceived and exquisitely inlaid birds, animals and monsters. A craftsman like Michel le Blon of Amsterdam knew that there was no nobler vehicle for his art than the stock of a gun which was likely to be treasured by one of the highest men in the land. Few things were more personal than a gun and few more truly individual. In the light of the exquisite quality of many of these arms it is a curious fact that we often do not know for whom they were made.

However, we do know who owned the pistols on page 39, which are the outstanding work of the gunmaker and watchmaker Pierre Bergier of Grenoble. They were made for Louis, Dauphin of France, later Louis XIV. In them we can see the art of the finest craftsmen. The barrels are beautifully damascened with gold and bear the royal motifs of the Crowned Dolphin and the crowned fleur-de-lis; the stocks are made from ebonised pear wood with mounts and furniture in gilt and damascened metal. The supreme skill of the contemporary engineer designer is also evident in the two-shot pistols which combine the superimposed load principle with waterproof wheel-locks. There is no doubt that by the time these pistols were made – somewhere between 1638 and 1643 – not only had the wheel-lock improved a great deal since Leonardo da Vinci's sketches, but also the entire concept of the hand gun as a portable and efficient part of the wardrobe had developed.

As with most major features of the developing gun there are a number of forms of the wheel-lock, yet most such locks have certain features in common. There is a steel wheel on a main shaft which is wound up by a key applied to the end of the shaft. In all of them a piece of iron pyrites is clamped in the cock and lowered on the wheel. The positioning of the wheel's edge in the bottom of the pan ensures that, on its rotating at high speed, the shower of sparks so generated cannot reasonably fail to ignite the powder. In later examples with self-spanning cocks and other refinements the wheel-lock is so efficient a mechanism that it really yields to the flintlock only for reasons of cost and fashion.

The oldest true flintlock comes from France. In the Hermitage Museum in Leningrad there is a flintlock gun made by Marin le Bourgeoys which is

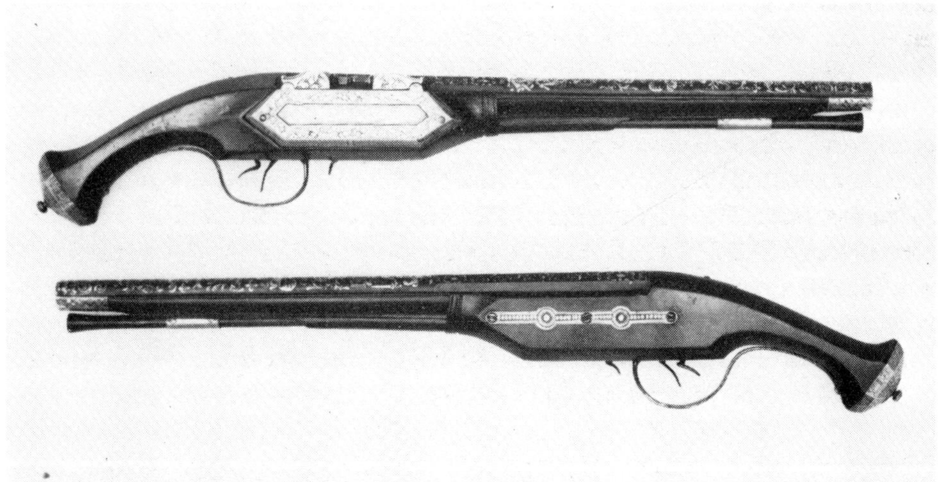

An example of the superimposed load, waterproof wheel-lock pistols by Pierre Bergier of Grenoble.

traditionally regarded as the property of Henry IV of France. It therefore dates from before 1610. Another one which was made for Louis XIII by Jean le Bourgeoys of Lisieux, in Normandy, must antedate 1615 as that is the year of its maker's death. Nevertheless, in spite of the early date of these royal arms, it was not until about 1640 that the flintlock began to be made outside France.

In a flintlock the sharp descent of a flint, held in the jaws of a cock, against a steel is the heart of the action. As the steel at its lower end becomes the pan cover, the pan remains covered until the split second that the flint, striking the steel, creates the sparks simultaneously flinging the cover and steel forward to clear the pan. It is difficult to determine to what extent the design of the flintlock stems directly from the wheel-lock, or to what extent it is directly descended from the snaphaunce. The latter was probably a Dutch invention of about 1540-50 and really differs from the later flintlock only in so far as the steel and pan cover were separate components. However, the cover could still be automatic in operation. In the snaphaunce the sear operated laterally through the lock plate to engage directly with the tail of the cock; whereas in the flintlock the sear operated vertically to engage half- and full-cock bents cut in the tumbler.

No chance was lost, in making these locks for the best guns, of finishing them in the finest fashion. The cock, especially, was chiselled in the most imaginative fashion. The comparative absence of mechanical parts on the outer face of the lock limited its treatment to a certain extent, but other variants of the flintlock, such as the miquelet in which the mainspring was exposed, offered wide freedom for chiselled decoration. The miquelet was very much the arm of Spain and north Africa, but it could still rival the arms of France and central Europe in its magnificent execution. The miquelet was not alone in being a regional or cultural variation on the general theme. As might be expected, locks and indeed treatments of the whole arm which show strong local and national trends occurred in countries as far apart as Scotland, Italy, Poland, Ceylon and Japan. Sometimes there is a petrification of type as in Japan, and in other cases, for example the agujeta of Ceylon, there seems to be a conscious denial of improving technical design for nationalistic reasons.

Fashion, as it affected the general treatment of the shape of such components as the lock plate or the cock and barrel, was very fickle. What was new in north Germany might be old in France. The adoption of the elegant swan neck cock slowly seemed to gain wide favour, and is one of the marks of a flintlock of later design. Less obviously, such improvements as the introduction of a detent in the lock to prevent its accidental discharge at half-cock – a French innovation of the late seventeenth century – are also marks of a later

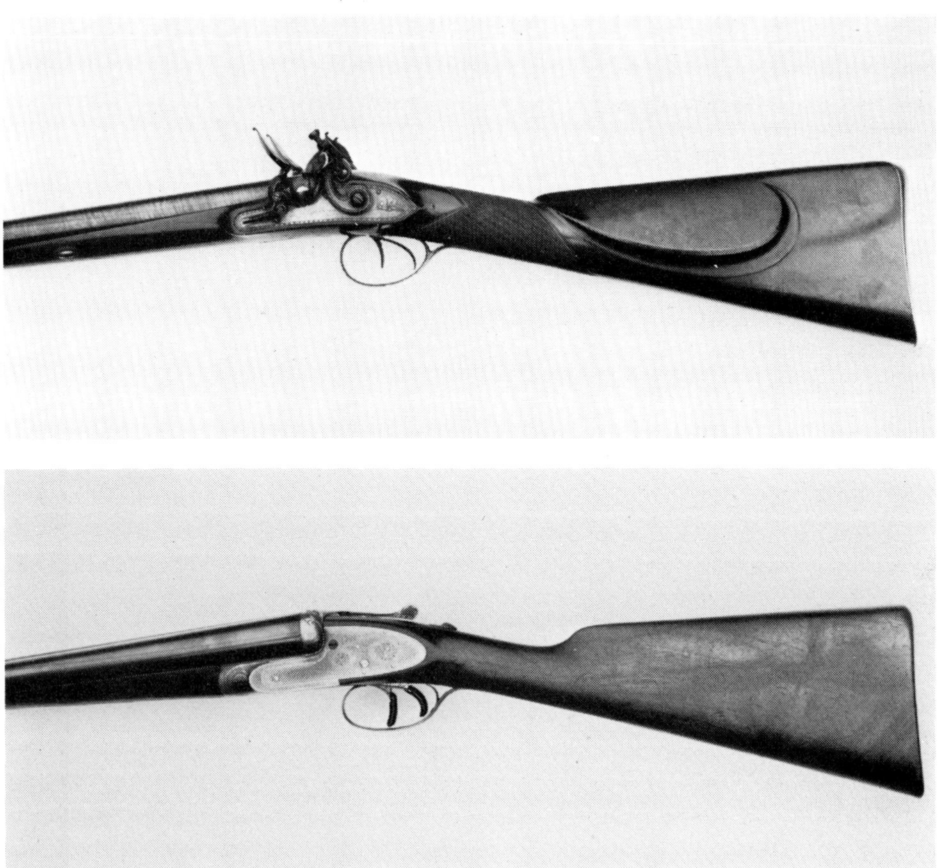

Top: 20 bore double-barrelled Manton shotgun c. 1805. Note the pronounced cheek piece, steel butt plate and general lightness of stocking.

Bottom: 12 bore double-barrelled Purdey shotgun preserving almost identical overall lines to the Manton of almost a century earlier.

and more sophisticated design. Various modifications to reduce friction in the operation of the mechanism must be included in this category, e.g. roller bearings at the point of contact between the steel and its spring, and a swivel link between main spring and tumbler.

The same sort of changes which affected the lock also influenced the development of the stock. When the early hand gun emerged in the form of an arquebus or musket which could be carried by one man, the stock was still very heavy. In the late sixteenth century a new style – the German – which had a stock which was much straighter and less flattened became popular. It was not until the late seventeenth century that a modern-looking stock finally appeared – the so-called French stock. It must be emphasised that these are only general trends and many stocks did not conform. Apart from regional and special arms, it was what the customer wanted which counted: in any age there are always some people who insist on asserting their individuality above all other considerations. Usually, but not always, this takes the form of clinging to older types and designs.

The stock's general form is only half the picture. There was its decoration also. Inlay of bone was a continuing fashion of the sixteenth-century stock-maker; not until about 1580 do we find the use of mother-of-pearl, but eventually this entirely supplanted bone. Then the wheel turned. In place of carving and inlay the seventeenth-century maker aimed to create something drawing its attraction simply from the quality of the wood and its overall shaping. Fashions are changeable. With the last quarter of the seventeenth century decorated stocks reappeared. There were at least two ways of achieving this. For the best arms silver mounts reflecting current artistic trends were fashionable. Carving and decorating the actual surface of the wood probably never became as popular as it had been in the sixteenth century, but certain features did emerge, including a carved pistol grip and, sometimes, cheek piece, and also the chequering of the small of the butt.

After the lock and stock comes the barrel. The Bergier pistols were not simply decorated in random fashion. The gold damascening on the barrels, as was customary in this period, followed exactly the designs in a pattern book by Thomas Picquot, *Livres de diverses ornaments de feuillages, moresques, grotesques, arabesque et autres inventions,* published in Paris in 1638. The aesthetic dominance of the barrel over the other components of the gun was established by the quality of the work of the great barrel-makers. No family was more celebrated in this direction than the Cominazzi of Brescia in Italy. It was no passing phenomenon. The Cominazzi were well known from the late sixteenth century until the nineteenth, although they reached the height of their international renown in the seventeenth century. The barrels they made are surprisingly light and attractive. The breech form is octagonal, but forward of the breech section, the barrel is rounded either with a slight central ridge or spirally fluted. The standing of the family's products was so high that they were exported to gunmakers all over Europe and even to England. The inevitable consequence was that today there are probably more faked 'Cominazzi' barrels than genuine articles!

Not all barrel-makers relied on chiselled steel. Some considered that the acme was reached by using solid silver, others employed brass, though this

Top: Gold inlay decoration on the lock plate of this late-19th-century German sporting rifle though simple in form could be very striking.

Bottom: Gold poincons, here carrying the famous name of Manton, inlet into the top of the patent breech and in front of the standing or false breech are usually to be found in the top-quality flintlock guns.

was normally for the strictly utilitarian purpose of minimising corrosion in arms intended for travelling or sea-service purposes. It was not until the 1770s that European makers began to produce the damascus barrels which today are regarded by most collectors as almost epitomising the fine arms of the past. However, once the technique appeared it soon became popular. Not only did it produce barrels which were light and very strong, but it also gave the more artistic makers scope to achieve very beautiful and intricate patterns in the metal. Basically, barrels of damascus or fine-twist type were constructed from separate rods of iron and steel heated and forged together, rolled and then twisted. Two or more of these compound bars were then welded together, rolled into a rod and flattened into a strip. It was this strip that was then wound in a spiral around an iron mandrel to be welded and hammered into the rough barrel. The final barrel, etched with acid to bring out the patterning, could be so handsome and was yet so practical that it must be a regret that no one today could make one.

The gun was more than the simple sum of lock, stock and barrel. It was often a work of art conceived and executed in every detail by artists and craftsmen of the highest standing. Thus nearly every possible technique of adornment can somewhere be found applied to guns. It could be encrusting, where, as in damascening, precious metal is inlaid but deliberately left proud; or enamelling; or etching; or even embossing. Inlay could take the more conventional form of inserting bone; of veneering; or it could be inletting silver wire, a style used in eighteenth-century England, where any art form lending itself to chinoiserie was always popular. The other way of approaching the complete gun was to give every part a closely integrated treatment in one medium. The Scottish all-metal pistol is perhaps the best-known example of this, but it was a dominant form for only a short period. Incidentally, it was not confined to Scotland.

Perhaps the French should be given credit for the creation of the finest arms ever made. Those that Nicholas Boutet, Director Artiste of the Imperial Factory at Versailles, made for Napoleon are unsurpassed in their exotic extravaganza. But for all their magnificence to many an eye they are no finer than the pair of saddle-holster pistols made by the La Roche for Louis XV of France. In these arms no trick was missed to dazzle the eye with a stunning mélange of blued and sculpted steel and gold. They are exactly what you might expect to be made for a king in the Galerie of the Louvre.

3

The Greatest Benefactor

One of the toughest matches in the Imperial Meeting at Bisley is the Armourers' match, last in a series of individual competitions which make up the aggregate for the Match Rifle Championship. After two sighters each competitor has to fire twenty counting shots at 1200 yards at a bullseye only twenty-four inches in diameter. Depending on his performance not only does each person know afterwards where he stands individually but also whether he has made it into his national team. It is particularly appropriate that the prize is a handsome, solid-silver medal commemorating the Reverend Alexander John Forsyth, arguably the greatest benefactor in the history of the development of firearms.

Forsyth, minister of Belhelvie in Scotland, was a keen wildfowler and thus particularly exasperated by the slow ignition of the charge in a flintlock. It was so slow, he wrote, that duck had time, on seeing the flash in the pan, to dive to safety underwater before there was any chance of the shot reaching them. The flintlock was not even fast enough in action to make shooting of flying birds very practical: consequently it was fully acceptable, indeed the norm, to shoot them sitting!

Unfortunately, speed was not the flintlock's only problem. The flint itself wore away with every shot. The sportsman who wished to be absolutely certain that his arm would not misfire had to change the flint after only about twelve shots, though usually thirty or forty shots could be safely taken. Even the face of the steel got chipped away and just occasionally would need refacing.

Obviously the flintlock was very vulnerable to rain or moisture. The introduction of a V-lipped pan, positioned so that no water could run straight into it, relieved the problem. However, it did not solve the entry of water between the inner lip of the pan cover and the side of the barrel; and just a little moisture in the powder could put the sportsman completely out of action. Unloading a soaked charge, with a screw on the end of the rammer

The Reverend Alexander Forsyth, inventor of the percussion system in 1807.

successively screwed into succeeding layers of the charge, was quite an operation: not to mention reloading and staying dry, all in heavy rain. With a double-barrelled shotgun there was the real danger of blowing your head off as you reloaded one barrel, when the other was still charged. It was very easy to forget to lower the cock on the loaded barrel in order to make it safe. A slight flaw in the engagement of the sear in the lock – quite a common fault – and the jar of ramming could fire the other barrel!

When a gun missed fire the sportsman's first instinct was not to draw the charge but to prick some more fine-grain powder through the vent, so that, if he were lucky, it would transmit the flame from the new powder in the pan to the powder of the charge. You were not, however, always lucky. If the cause was simply that too much powder had been placed in the pan, and this had become caked and relatively inert under the pressure of the pan cover, the remedy was obvious. So it was, too, if the flint had become loose in the jaws of the cock – it should, ideally, be clamped between leather but lead would do. More rarely, when a badly-cleaned gun was put away for some time, the touch hole became corroded and closed up. This risk was much reduced with platinum bouching around the touch hole, a feature of good guns by the late eighteenth-century. Yet in spite of these faults the flintlock still represented an appreciable advance over most that had gone before.

Forsyth was not only a keen sportsman but he was also a keen amateur student of chemistry and engineering. Initially, he felt that the solution to his problems might be found in improving the strength of the gunpowder. He thought that by substituting suitable fulminates for all or part of the potassium nitrate he would achieve his objective. He was, however, still using spark ignition. We do not know exactly when or how the idea occurred, but he eventually realised that all he needed to do to ignite the charge was to strike or percuss the powder. His next step was to design a lock to make this possible. So the famous 'scent bottle' or roller magazine lock was born. In principle it was simplicity itself. The scent bottle contained a supply of five grains of percussion powder. A small plug in the cover closure of the magazine provided a safety vent in the unlikely event of the flash from a shot passing round a worn pivot to the magazine. The scent bottle was simply rotated 180° on its axis so that, by gravity, one eighth of a grain of powder dropped into a little anvil cavity on top of it. The magazine was then returned to its usual position so that the striker was over the anvil. All that was then necessary was to pull the trigger, releasing the hammer to hit the striker. The snag was that such a lock required very fine workmanship and materials which made it rather expensive. It was an excellent solution for the wealthy sportsman but rather less so for the soldier.

The flint and the steel were both subject to appreciable wear: the former needed changing after somewhere between a dozen and three dozen shots, the latter refacing occasionally if the gun was used heavily.

In good-quality guns the communication between the pan and the charge was bouched with platinum which alone seemed able to stand up without appreciable enlargement of the vent to the great heat and pressures generated.

Forsyth's lock certainly proved itself in the field. It was fast to prime and virtually instantaneous in ignition – as fast in fact as a modern cartridge gun. No duck could dive that fast! But like most inventors he was not content. He continued to experiment in his smithy, a garden house, in the grounds of Belhelvie and eventually produced a modified design, where the priming was effected automatically by cocking the hammer. It still used loose powder and so it retained all the disadvantages of a very dangerous and unstable substance – that is if it were handled in bulk. Nevertheless, Forsyth's lock represented an enormous improvement over previous systems, and it naturally followed that it was investigated for military use. It had worked so well through the wildfowling season in 1805-6 that Forsyth decided to go to London and show the entire gun to Lord Moira, Master General of the Ordnance. He was sufficiently impressed to provide Forsyth at the Tower with all the workshop facilities he needed to develop a more durable version of his lock for military purposes. Indeed he even secured for him the necessary leave of absence from his ecclesiastical duties. Forsyth responded enthusiastically, producing versions of his lock for both musket and cannon, together with improved fulminating powder. But unfortunately at the critical juncture Lord Chatham, brother of William Pitt the Prime Minister, succeeded as MGO, and apparently took against Forsyth and his work. It was the end of a great opportunity when Britain could have taken a giant stride ahead of the rest of Europe in the efficiency of her armament. Forsyth and all his experimental arms were ejected from the Tower.

It is quite surprising that Forsyth was still sufficiently patriotic to refuse a French offer of £20,000 for his invention – at least that is the tradition – but perhaps he thought that all military authorities were likely to be tarred with the same brush. Instead he concentrated on the release of his lock to the public.

In 1807 he protected his invention with patent No. 3032. This was so effective that there was really no serious opposition to him in Britain until after its expiry in 1821. He had been helped in securing this patent by James Watt, the inventor of the steam engine, and by James Purdey, a gunmaker. The business of selling guns with his lock was established at No. 10 Piccadilly and soon it became the mecca for the forward-looking sportsman. Any money which Forsyth made came from this business – at his death he had received from the British authorities only £200 for his invention, which by then was carried by almost every soldier.

Logically, the next step forward in the development of the design of the perfect firearm was to have the percussion-ignition element contained in the cartridge and to load it from the breech. In addition to reducing the risk of blowing your head off or, in the case of the soldier skirmishing, to minimising the chance of being shot while loading, loading at the breech eliminated the wear made by the rammer on the muzzle. There is probably no factor or feature of a gun that contributes more to accuracy than the regularity of the muzzle's form. With a worn muzzle the gases escape irregularly around the ball or bullet, so that the actual direction in which the projectile departs becomes quite random.

A self-contained cartridge was invented by Jean Samuel Paully. More than that, he designed and manufactured a very advanced pattern of breech loader to handle it. It would not have been technically successful if the cartridges had allowed an escape of gas at the breech. By using brass, Paully anticipated the modern solution to the problem of obturating or sealing the breech. With brass there is a momentary expansion of the case which seals the breech, followed by a sufficient degree of contraction to allow it to be extracted easily after firing. Paully was at least half a century ahead of his time. Thoughtfully he cased his guns with all the necessary tools and other items, so that his client could load and reload his cartridge cases as necessary.

Jean Samuel Paully secured a French patent for his invention in September 1812. Though Swiss, at the time of the granting of his patent he had been working in Paris for about four years. About 1814 he quit Paris and came to England but, while many examples of his extraordinarily advanced arms exist, he so failed to make a commercial success of his invention that we do not even know exactly where or when he died. 1828 is the best guess that can be made.

It is impossible to exaggerate the forward-looking character of Paully's invention. He covered by patents both cartridges with short brass bases and those with long brass cylindrical forms, very similiar to those used today. Admittedly the percussion element took the form of a small pellet, in effect, of percussion powder, which was seated in a steel-lined recess in the centre of the exterior of the base of the case. But when the striker detonated it, the flash communicated with the charge in the body of the cartridge via a fine hole just as it does in a modern centre fire cartridge. The quality and efficacy of the design of his gun to handle these cartridges were equally of the first order. Almost the only possible form of misuse to which his gun could be subjected – and the user would need to be extraordinarily negligent – was to confuse the priming with the propellant powder. At least he would do it only once – if he survived at all, his injuries would almost certainly be so serious he would not be able to do it again!

The defect, if there were one, in both Forsyth and Paully's systems was the vulnerability of the percussion powder. It seemed to many that prepackaging of the fulminate was what was needed. This would, and in fact did, take almost any form. One of the earliest was the patch – the fulminate was encased between two discs of waterproof sealed paper. Amongst other vehicles for the fulminate were tubes, pills, pellets and caps. Judged against Forsyth's system they really represented an appreciable technical advance only where they preserved the magazine feature in addition to gaining in safety and certainty in adverse climatic conditions. That is a twentieth-century judgement: what actually happened was that one type of percussion lock – the caplock – slowly drove most other forms off the market. Whilst copper percussion caps *could* be magazine-loaded and indeed were in some experimental arms, or could at least be seated by means of a capper, in fact they rarely were.

Yet arms using percussion caps – later caps were extremely waterproof – were adopted by most of the armies of Europe, not least by the British. Because the authorities were so reluctant, largely for financial reasons, to do the job properly, British soldiers who had to handle percussion caps in extreme cold, in Canada for example, had great difficulty. The question that naturally arises is who first thought of the idea of copper caps or thimbles? There is no lack of claimants for the honour.

Colonel Peter Hawker, the eminent sportsman and author of probably the best known treatise on shooting, *Instructions to Young Sportsmen*, is one of the many claimants, but so too were the gunmakers, Egg and Purdey. In American eyes Joshua Shaw was such a strong contender that he was awarded £4000 – incidentally, a mere £2800 more than Forsyth and his family after his death received in total for the master invention! Although by the 1840s the

Purdey's military muzzle-loading musket (c. 1850) of a type said to have been carried by some local levies.

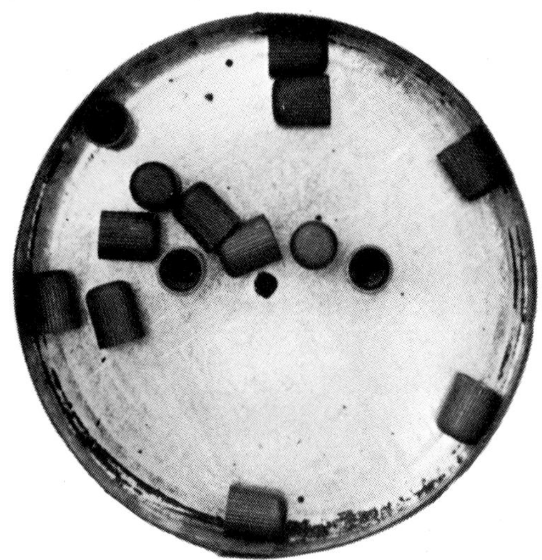

Percussion caps were made in the 19th century in differing qualities. These are ones in heavy-gauge copper intended for match rifle use.

copper cap was generally triumphant, it was perhaps most challenged by the tube. One of the earliest and most successful of these was invented by Joseph Manton in 1818. The tubelock was especially successful on the Continent where, in some cases, it remained the chosen percussion form of lock mechanism until superseded by the breechloader. Even in England Colonel Peter Hawker found a tubelock design patented by Westley Richards in 1811 to be surprisingly reliable under all weather conditions.

Today, it is a very enjoyable pursuit to be a collector of early percussion systems, because there were, and still are, so many variations. For those who dealt in arms and whose prime task was to keep their customers happy, it cannot always have been easy to have in stock the appropriate percussion initiator. Some types were distinctly dangerous. The amount of fulminate composition in some, and the likelihood of accidental explosion, could not be overlooked. The copper cap compared favourably with most other vehicles, though it had a disconcerting habit of flying badly when manufactured from sheet copper of too thin a gauge. In extreme cases the firer's eyes were in real danger.

By the 1840s, whether national or otherwise, the percussion cap was dominant, and through it Forsyth's invention reigned supreme. Only the sailors of the Royal Navy, as spent caps embedded themselves in their bare feet, had mixed feelings, and their complaint, after all, was not against Forsyth himself. Forsyth at least lived to see the new era he had initiated firmly established, as he did not die until June 1843.

4

Riflemen Form

In all the vast number of firearms which have been successively launched on to mankind very few can be described as epoch-making. Usually, as in the introduction of a new form of lock, the transition is so subtle that it is not possible to spotlight a single weapon. For this reason it is particularly exciting to be able to pinpoint a weapon which really marks a watershed between the old and the new.

The arrival on the European scene in the 1840s of a rifle which relied upon the self-expanding bullet was truly epoch-making. The most famous system was that of Delvigne-Minié which manifested itself in Britain as the Pattern 1851 rifled musket. Fortunately its manufacture was put in hand just in time to ensure that, soon after the outbreak of the Crimean War in 1854, most of the line regiments involved were equipped with them.

The main characteristic of the 1851 rifled musket is a barrel of .702″ calibre rifled with four concentric grooves to spin the bullet: the bullet was well below the barrel in diameter so that it was easily loaded at the muzzle and rammed home. The exploding charge provided the agency for expanding the bullet to fit the bore and thus to take the rifling; ignition of the charge was by a percussion caplock. The accuracy expected from the rifle was such that it needed a long tangent backsight graduated to 900 yards – nor was this for show. The rifle was so much longer ranged than any of its predecessors that both soldiers and the authorities were at times taken unaware. Dead cows on Plumstead Marshes were the earliest reminders of its potency at long range!

To modern eyes the Pattern '51 rifle musket is an incredibly simple weapon. So it is even more difficult to take in the extent of its superiority over its predecessors when outwardly it looks so similar. The critical features – the devastating novelty – are in the long tradition that the really great advances are usually so simple that one cannot understand why they were not invented sooner. Essentially the P'51 marked a great step forward because it used a new

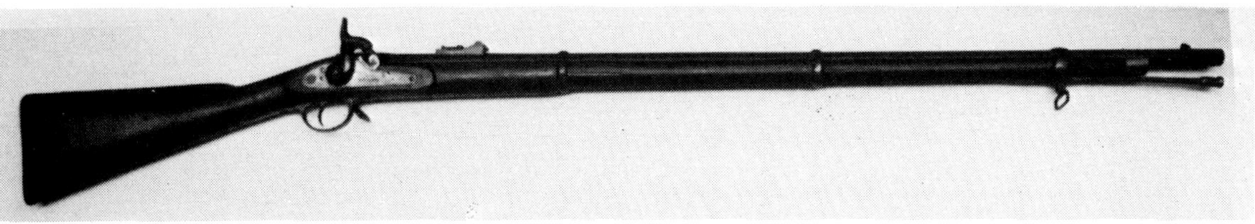

For over ten years from 1854 onward the .577 P '53 Enfield muzzle-loading military rifle and the .450 Whitworth were bitter rivals for the favour of the British authorities. The Enfield won but the Whitworth was extensively tested in troop trials and in the models of 1862 and 1863 saw very limited issue.

form of ammunition. This performed very well largely because by the 1850s manufacturing tolerances were sufficiently tight to be able to adhere to the right relationship of bore and bullet diameters. It helped that the rifle had a form of rifling compatible with getting reasonable accuracy and a reduced calibre, which also assisted in achieving a stiffer and more predictable barrel through a better ratio of wall thickness to bore diameter.

It took a number of years for the armies of Europe to harness the new form of rifle musket to the most lethal effect. Although this was the rifle's real début on the world stage, there had been rifles – albeit in military terms very different kettles of fish – in military issue, even in England, for almost a hundred years.

The British army in the 1750s made little use of the rifle but a few, apparently of German Jaeger style, were used by it for fighting the Indians in America. With the outbreak of the American War of Independence these same rifles were turned upon the British. The new situation produced a swift response from the British – they ordered 1000 rifles, 200 from Germany and 800 from Birmingham. Most of these arms were probably never delivered. On the other hand, the British rifle of which so much is heard, was that designed by Captain Ferguson of the 70th Regiment. In April 1776 he demonstrated it to the authorities who were so impressed that the order for the muzzle-loading rifles was countermanded and Ferguson rifles substituted. Within the year a hundred of the new breechloading rifles had been made and were on issue to troops for training. The new rifle, capable of at least four rounds a minute, performed very well in action. Ferguson himself was wounded at the Battle of Brandywine. When he recovered he went on to distinguish himself in subsequent engagements until, at the Battle of King's Mountain on 7 October 1780, he was killed. Without his advocacy and example, his rifle vanished from the military scene. Ironically, posterity remembers the muzzle-loading Kentucky rifle carried by so many of the American irregulars even more enthusiastically than the screw breech Ferguson. In fact, far the most common

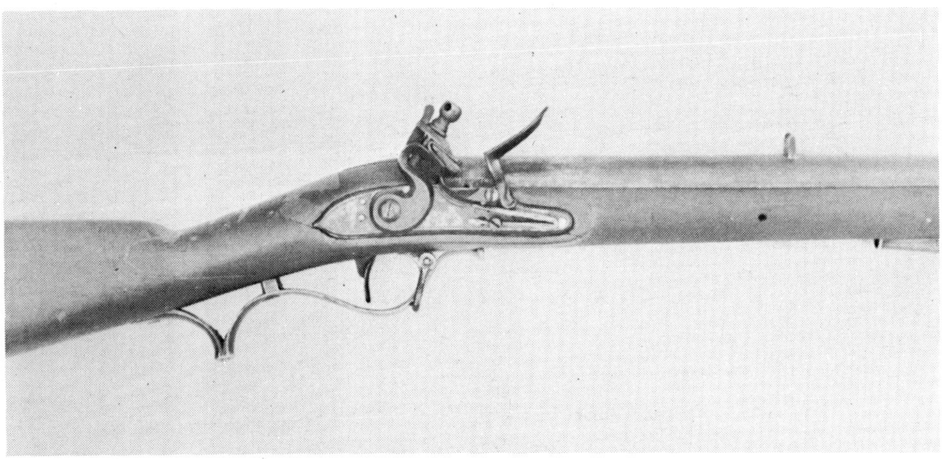

Baker rifle by Henry Nock for Cambridge University Volunteers, with conventional flintlock, c. 1805.

firearm, in both the British and American Forces, was the flintlock smoothbore musket.

The taste for rifles lingered in British military circles. In 1785, only five years after Ferguson's death, a few experimental breechloading rifles were issued to some regiments of the Light Dragoons. Interestingly, until the 1790s the rifle in British Military service, so far as it *was* found, was breechloading and, of course, experimental. During the 1790s, however, the muzzle-loading rifle, long favoured on the Continent, began to gain favour in Britain. A few were made for military use in England but, in 1798, 5000 were ordered in Prussia. These were of such poor quality that the British authorities, increasingly convinced of the wisdom of establishing a Rifle Corps, set about finding a supply in England.

It was this trial, in February 1800, that was won by a London gunmaker, Ezekiel Baker, and very soon afterwards 800 Baker rifles were ordered. In the face of the threat from France, the British had at last decided to manufacture their own rifle in a reasonable quantity. They were, however, producing rifles for riflemen, not ordinary soldiers. Their proper use was too demanding and the difficulties of loading too great for them to be widely adopted. That was the view of rifles taken by commanders like Wellington, and it justifiably remained the official view for many more decades.

Baker's rifle is by no means common today and is quite a collector's piece. It was set up with a barrel .625″ in calibre, rifled with seven grooves making a quarter turn in its 30″ length. This slow twist was satisfactory for accuracy at

Shooting medals of the Napoleonic Wars serve as a mine of information upon dress, weapons, targets, stance, etc.

For a period of over fifty years, until the 1820s, shooting medals, generally of silver, were awarded to the best shot in the regiment. They are as attractive to the present-day collector as they were to the original recipient who was allowed to wear it on his uniform.

short ranges and helped to keep down fouling, but it did not perform so well at longer distances. Yet, for all its limitations, the Baker was adopted by many of the thousands who combined to meet the threat of Napoleon. There are records of some amazing feats of marksmanship with it. A good shot who was prepared to load with great care and fortunate enough to have a rifle in very good condition could hit a 12″ circle nearly every time at 200 yards. We know, both from contemporary printed records and from some of the silver medals which were awarded to the regimental 'best shots', that Baker rifles were occasionally even shot at 300 yards in competition. A great deal can be gleaned about the various firing positions and conditions under which riflemen competed from these usually most handsome and attractive engraved medals.

The Baker rifle was sufficiently efficient for serious efforts to replace it to be initiated only when it became clear that it had to be superseded. If British riflemen were to preserve basic parity with their Continental opposite numbers, they would have to carry percussion arms. The two-grooved, percussion Brunswick rifle began to replace the Baker in 1837. The new arm had a barrel of .654″ calibre with rifling making a single turn in the length of the barrel. The muzzle ends of the two large grooves were notched so that the riflemen could locate them in the dark. For the bullet, a ball, was made with a raised belt around it that mechanically engaged the rifling. The ball was enveloped in a greased linen patch and loaded on top of a 2¼ drams blank powder charge. The loading procedure, with the precisely fitting bullet, was quite time-consuming: in an emergency situation the rifleman was permitted to fire ordinary cartridges with 17 bore spherical ball. These were a loose fit and could be loaded and fired much more rapidly, although accuracy was almost completely sacrificed.

A heavy version of the Brunswick rifle in an amazing .796″ calibre was manufactured in 1840 for the Navy, for sniping at officers on enemy ships. It was the first British military small arm to be fitted with a complex sight. In comparison with the improvement that the P'51 rifled musket represented over what had gone before, however, both the Heavy Navy rifle and the Brunswick were scarcely more accurate than the arm they supplanted.

Many have tried to discover the true inventor of the self-expanding or, indeed, the expanding bullet but nothing has been proved. One contender is Captain Norton of the British army who appears to have suggested the idea about 1818; another is Lt Col. Davidson who produced a number of different patterns of expanding bullet in 1832. Three years later William Greener, a Birmingham gunmaker, suggested a compound expanding bullet, but it seems that one of the earliest successful approaches to the problem was made by a Frenchman, Thouvenin. He fixed a pillar in the breech, projecting

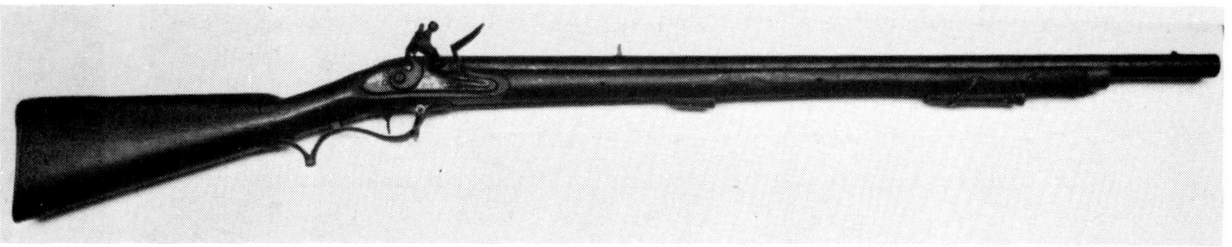

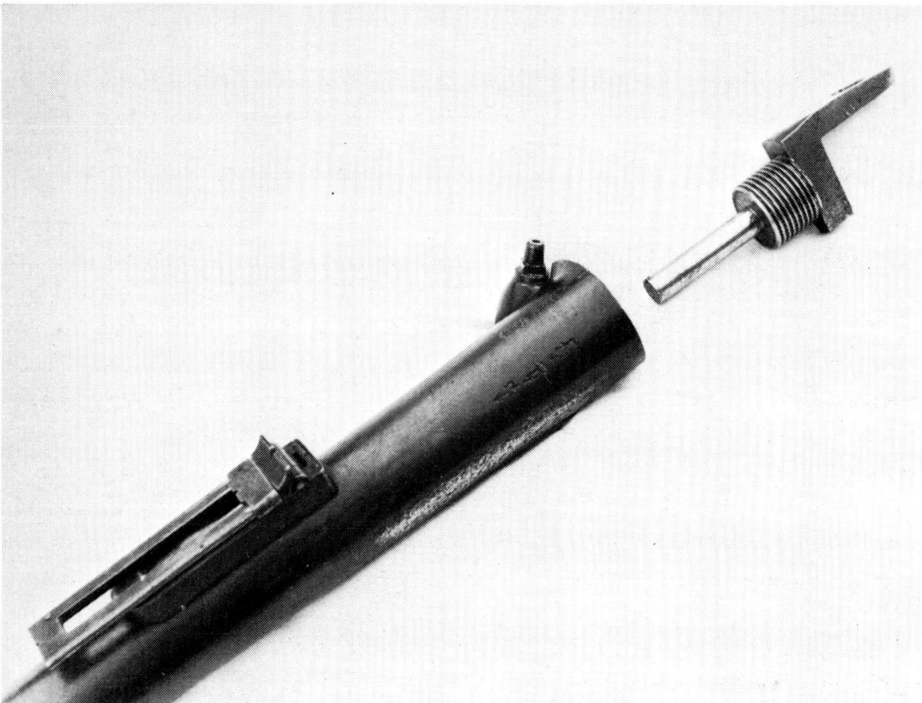

In the first decades of the 19th century Riflemen were highly specialised troops. The flintlock Baker rifle (*top*) was first introduced into the Rifle Corps in 1800. This arm fired spherical ball ammunition with little accuracy beyond about 250 yards.

The tige or pillar breech unscrewed from an Enfield experimental rifle specially manufactured to assess this French system.

Bullets with cannelures for the lubricant and as an aid for expansion through 'telescoping'. The upper one, however, relied for expansion on a base cavity.

parallel to the bore from the breech face so that the last strokes of ramming the bullet to the bottom of the barrel and against the pillar literally expanded the bullet to fit the rifling grooves. The great drawback was that after ramming no two bullets were likely to be exactly the same in shape, so accuracy was impaired.

Two other Frenchmen, Delvigne and Minié, made the real breakthrough. In their design, expansion was achieved by the outwards wedging action of an iron cup in the base of the bullet. Later it was realised that exactly the same effect could be attained by simply providing the bullet with a base cavity – the exploding gases inside it would do all that was needed. Later still, it was appreciated that the mere mass of the bullet contributed to expansion, in that the inertia of the front of the bullet led to the rear of the bullet expanding sideways, in attempting to overtake it, so no base cavity was needed. The Delvigne-Minié system first reached the British soldier in the shape of the P'51 rifle musket – so called because it was no longer the rifle of an élite corps but the general arm of the soldier. In this way red remained the colour of the uniform – if every soldier had been translated into a rifleman scarlet would have yielded to dark green and few, least of all the Duke of Wellington, wanted that!

In one important respect the rifle musket remained firmly attached to the past. The bullet, required by the Duke of Wellington to weigh at least one ounce, actually weighed 680 grains, almost $1\frac{1}{2}$ ounces. When the Great Duke died in 1852 the real obstacle to reduction in the size of the bore was removed. A smaller-calibre arm with smaller bullets would enable the soldier to carry more ammunition for the same gross weight.

Trials held at Enfield in 1852 led to the selection of a new calibre as the optimum for the new British rifle musket, the .577". At the same time four grooves, which had the theoretical disadvantage of allowing simultaneous expansion of the bullet at diametrically opposed points and therefore loss of desirable ballistic form, were dropped in favour of three. It scarcely needed these changes to enhance the performance of the arm. The Pattern 1851 rifle musket performed amazingly in the Crimean War. As *The Times* correspondent wrote, 'The volleys of the Minié cleft them like the hand of the Destroying Angel, and they fell like leaves in autumn before them.'

Yet there was a change which could, and did, appreciably improve the shooting of the rifle musket – of the permanent supersession of the conoidal bullet by one of cylindro-conoidal form. William Metford, later celebrated above all other British arms designers of the nineteenth century, replaced the bullet with box wood cup by one with a small base cavity, the so-called Pritchett bullet. The bullet was lubricated by means of its waxed paper

This famous picture of Edward Ross, the first winner of the Queen's prize at Wimbledon in 1860, excellently conveys the appearance of the firing points and the atmosphere of competition.

wrapping which was self-discarding at the muzzle. The Swiss system of containing the lubricant in deep grooves or cannelures around the bullet, so that it squeezed out with their compression on firing, was never adopted in Britain for the muzzle-loading rifle musket.

The new reduced bore .577 rifle musket, the Pattern of 1853, had a long and very distinguished career. Carried in the last battles of the Crimea and in the Indian Mutiny, they were probably the most widely used rifles in the American Civil War. They were manufactured not only at Enfield, in London and in Birmingham, but even on contract at Liège, St Etienne, and in Vermont in the USA. Some of these contract rifles are rare and very much sought after by collectors but none had the superb appearance and finish of those marked 'Enfield'.

The Pattern '53 rifle musket became the parent of a whole family of arms. According to the original official inventories, by 1862 there were no fewer than seventy-two patterns of small arms simultaneously in service in the

FN M 1924 version of the M 98 Mauser rifle.

An HBSA range practice with breech-loading rifles. Nearest to camera the .303 Long Lee Enfield Service rifle of the Boer War.

Firing a .577 muzzle-loading P '53 Enfield rifle musket in the annual Oxford and Cambridge match at Bisley.

The Rifle Contest, Wimbledon, 1864.

The Final of HM The Queen's Prize at Bisley in the 1960s.

'Blowing off' to foul the bore at the beginning of a distance, in the Cambridge Cup at Barton Road Range.

British forces. The great majority of them were of the Delvigne-Minié type derived from the outstanding P'53.

There is no doubt that the P'53 was built to the right formula, but there was nothing magical about its composition. For example, three-groove rifling was very nearly abandoned in favour of oval-bore rifling. In fact, it was such a close contender that it was adopted for the arms of the Royal Engineers. Nor is it accurate to see the P'53 as having vanquished rifles which relied upon a mechanically-fitting bullet. Colonel Jacob's deep, four-grooved rifle, which shot so very well in the 1850s in India at extreme long range, and Joseph Whitworth's polygonally-bored rifles of the 1850s and 1860s, immediately spring to mind. Both remained competitors, but for all their merits neither ever seriously threatened the dominance of the P'53.

The P'53 also became the principal arm of the Volunteers who, increasingly after 1859 with the threat of invasion from France, met and organised themselves in units and to shoot. It was, perhaps, ironical that the royal accolade when it came – Queen Victoria agreed to fire the first shot to inaugurate the National Rifle Association's first meeting in 1860 at Wimbledon – was for the Whitworth rather than the Enfield. There are some of us who feel that the Enfield – the P'53 – might have placed its shot at 400 yards within one inch of dead centre of the target! There are many present-day enthusiasts, who make a serious sport out of shooting the P'53, who would have little doubt about this!

5
A Close Companion

It was a very long time before the pistol was accepted as a serious military weapon. Not until the closing decades of the nineteenth century could this be said to be true. To be acceptable to an officer in the field it had to be high-powered and to have a multi-shot capacity. The kind of high-powered, 10-shot Mauser pistol which the young Winston Churchill carried in Africa was certainly a military weapon, but its design had emerged only after a long, painful period of gestation.

Probably the most successful of early methods tried to achieve multi-shot capacity was rotation – rotating a cylinder so that loaded chambers were brought in succession into alignment with the barrel. There were other methods. The most obvious was multiplying the number of barrels – the last and perhaps most successful pistols with more than two barrels were the Lancaster four-barrelled pistols of the late nineteenth century. There were magazine systems handling loose powder and balls but these were always expensive and never very reliable, even when made by such notable makers as Caspar Kalthoff and Harman Barnes. This early kind of magazine system and the superimposed-load mode were both rarely applied to pistols.

If the celebrated Puckle gun in the Tower is discounted as being the 'revolving' system applied to a larger arm, it is not until the very late eighteenth century that a serious pattern of flintlock revolving pistol is found. Captain Wheeler of Concord, Mass., is usually credited with the earliest practical design but credit for producing the first really successful revolver pistol should go to Elisha Collier of Boston, Mass. Although based on Wheeler's design, Collier's main improvements were the mechanical rotation of the cylinder on cocking, and the self priming of the pan.

With the advent of the percussion lock as an established feature of the gun, the design problem of the revolver was somewhat simplified. Soon the pepperbox revolver, where there is no main barrel but each chamber is a barrel

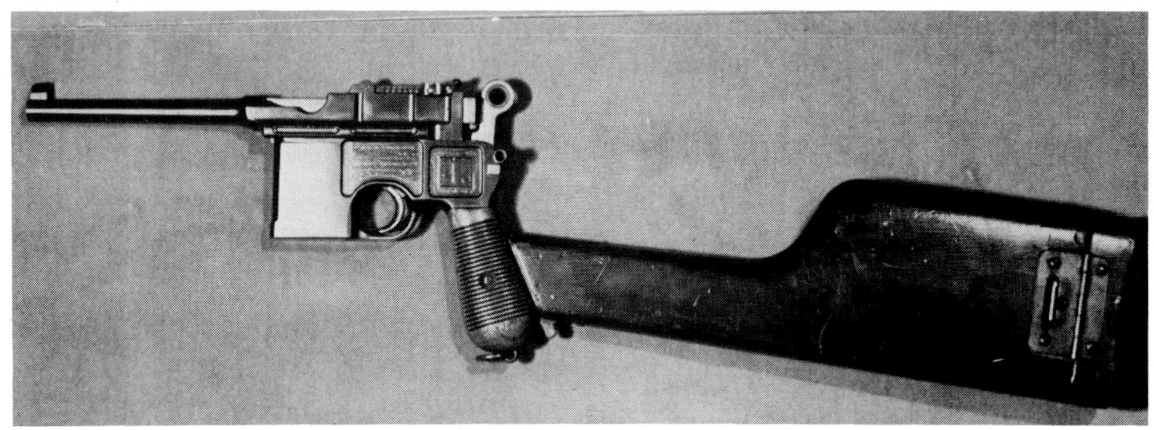

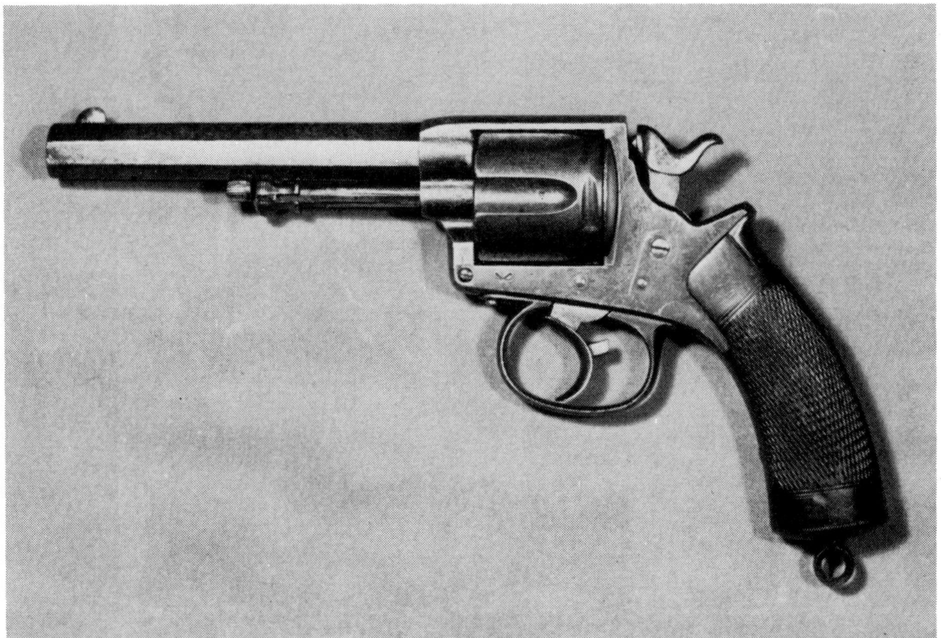

Top: An arm which may fairly be called epoch making and was the first really commercially successful semi-automatic pistol. The Mauser model of 1896 here seen with its holster stock attached for carbine use.

Bottom: The .45 Adams service revolver passed through three marks or major design changes. All had rod ejections and loaded single cartridges into the chamber through a gate which necessitated turning the cylinder to align each chamber in turn with it.

in its own right, was being turned out by all classes of maker. One of the most common of these, called the Mariette, was patented in Belgium in 1837. Over fifty British makers produced pepperboxes, including such well-known names as Westley Richards, Joseph Lang, Cooper, and Tipping and Lawden. Pepperboxes achieved such popularity that they survived for many years alongside conventional revolvers, though it was a disadvantage that the barrels of the large bores were very heavy. Perhaps they held on to their popularity against apparent expectation because they were safer than the true muzzle-loading revolver in one important way. With a revolver it was possible for the flash from the discharge of one chamber to penetrate past the bullet in adjacent chambers and cause a chain explosion. When this occurred the bullets from the chambers not in alignment with the barrel smashed into the frame, and in a large-bore weapon this had distinctly unpleasant consequences for the firer and those standing on either side.

To avoid all risk of premature discharge the revolver had to be loaded carefully and correctly with properly-fitted and lubricated bullets. This took time and the operation was not completed until each nipple had been capped. Even the legendary Colt used this system, for Colt's genius lay not so much in original design as in the successful application of machinery to quantity-production of arms, together with knowing how to sell them.

Though Colt's production began in 1836 at Paterson, in New Jersey, it was on a very small scale. In 1842 he went into liquidation and, though he restarted, it was not until the late 1840s that he had produced sufficient arms to make any great impact. When he encountered Adams, the first really successful British revolver designer and maker, at the Great Exhibition of 1851, Colt was just beginning to be successful.

The 1851 model of the Adams revolver was the only British product which could compete with the unquestionably efficient Colt. With its solid frame and integral top-strap above the cylinder, the Adams was much stronger than the Colt, and was its equal in accuracy. In most ways it was the better military weapon.

The Colt Navy Model of 1851, in .36 calibre, was a lighter and therefore more widely portable arm. It was well finished and not without appeal. Indeed Colt was so sure of his success that he even opened a factory in London and issued invitations to the public to visit. It was undoubtedly an enormous social success, as well as being a milestone in the development of mechanised production of arms where its influence was profound. Everybody visited the factory, which became one of the sights of London and remained so until it was closed in 1857.

Colt lost no opportunity for presenting fine examples of his arms to

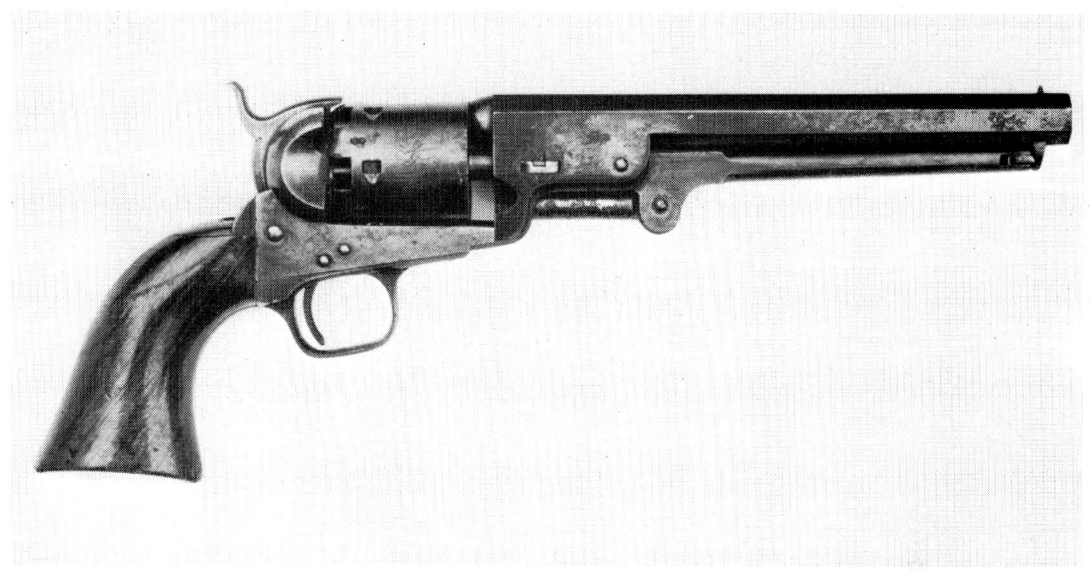

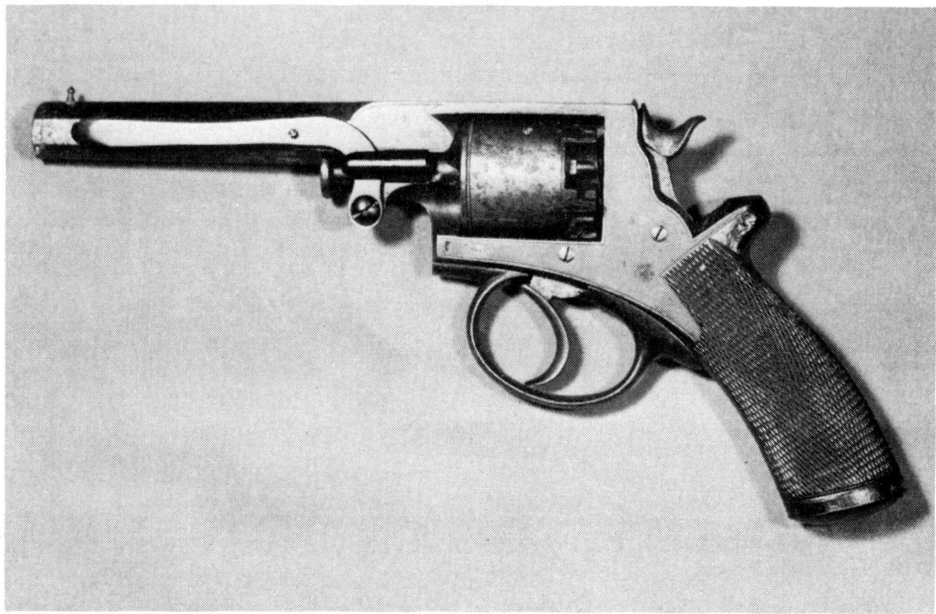

Top: .36 Colt Navy Model Revolver. This weapon was said to have been presented to Lord Lucan during the Crimean War.

Bottom: The .45 Beaumont Adams muzzle-loading revolver was so successful as to be fairly widely issued in the British forces. Amongst its notable features were the solid frame and top strap and an excellent single- and double-action trigger mechanism.

prominent public figures. One Navy revolver was presented to Lord Lucan of Crimean fame: it was this pattern which he persuaded the British authorities to order for the Royal Navy in 1854. They bought 9500, and a year later a further 14,000 were bought by the Board of Ordnance for issue to the army.

It looked as though Colt had everything wrapped up, but Adams came back and slowly his revolver and then others of the same general type succeeded in radically containing the Colt invasion. The muzzle-loading revolver was a fully established member of the military arms family, and yet, even before the 1850s were out, the days of any type of muzzle-loading revolver were numbered.

In 1855 two Americans, Horace Smith and Daniel B. Wesson, having acquired the rights of Rollin White's patent of 1855 for a bored-through cylinder, produced the first popular and successful breechloading cartridge revolver in .22. The .22 rimfire cartridge actually dates from about 1854 though the earliest rimfire cartridges go back to at least 1846. As Smith and Wesson held on to the Rollin White patent until 1869 the obvious way to breechloading was blocked to every other American maker. Although powerful cartridges with a rim distribution of fulminate are unacceptable because of the high risk of the rim rupturing, there was no technical difficulty in producing low-powered rimfire cartridges in .32, and later in .41 and other calibres.

In parallel with the American development of the rimfire cartridge, there was the French invention, by Lefauchaux in 1854, of the pinfire cartridge. The original invention dates from 1828 and therefore considerably antedates the American. It is remarkable that pinfire cartridges remained in limited production until the Second World War. The French authorities took a long time to capitalise their national advantage, and it was not until 1856, after they had tried both the Colt and the Adams revolvers, that they adopted Lefauchaux's pinfire revolver. In 1858 the Italians followed suit and the Scandinavian countries in 1864. Other countries, including Britain, considered that it was not safe enough to adopt, since the exposed pin could be accidentally struck and the cartridge detonated. So both of these early systems had their intrinsic disadvantages – what everyone was waiting for was a safe and durable centre-fire, self-contained cartridge.

It was in 1858 that Pottet produced a successful gas-tight, centre-fire, shotgun cartridge case, but it was some years before a good revolver case was made. The breakthrough in revolvers came with John Adams's .450 double-action, breechloading pattern of 1867, which the army adopted in 1868. Further models followed in 1871 and 1878. With these well-designed and

Top: .22 rimfire Smith and Wesson model of 1857 pocket revolver.

Bottom: Military calibre pinfire revolvers of very good quality were made by a number of Continental makers. This by Javelle of St Etienne has a number of attractive features.

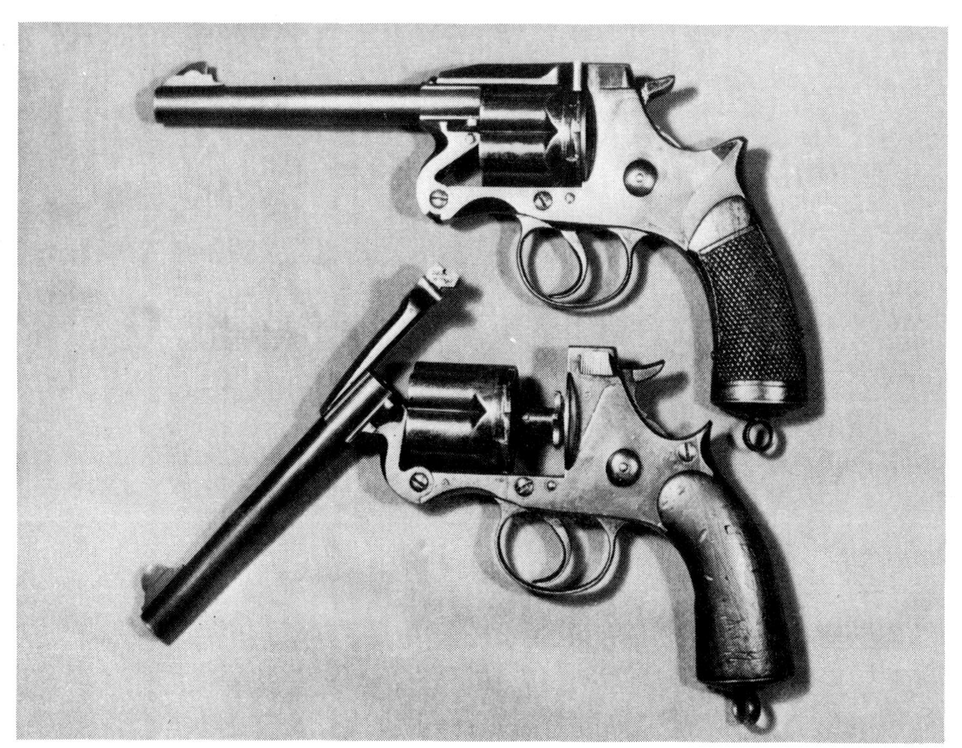

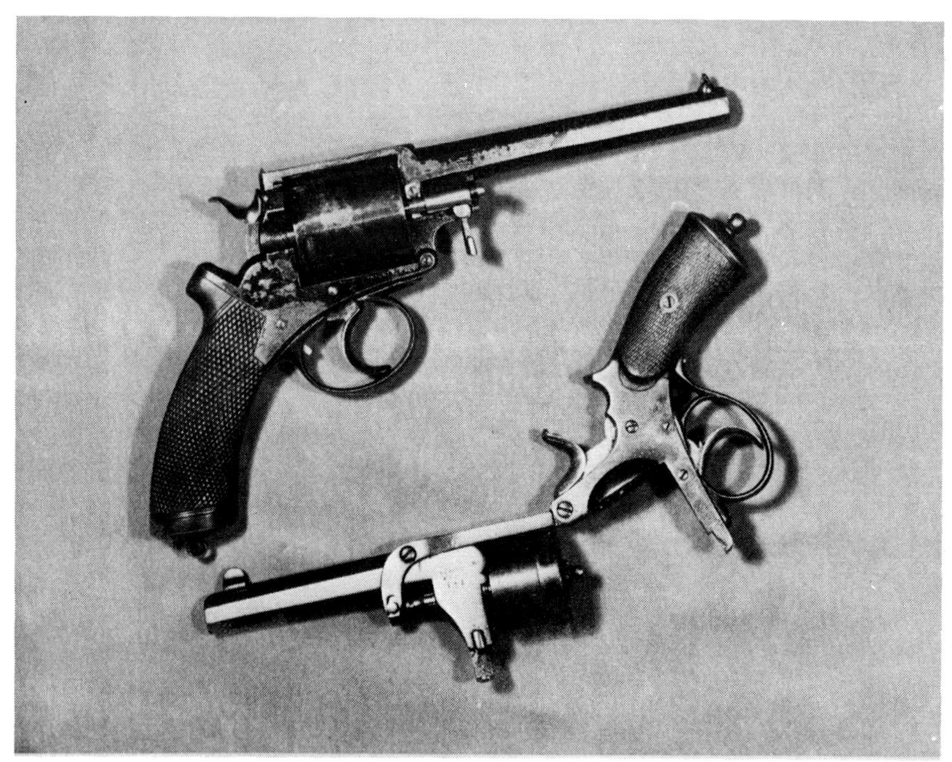

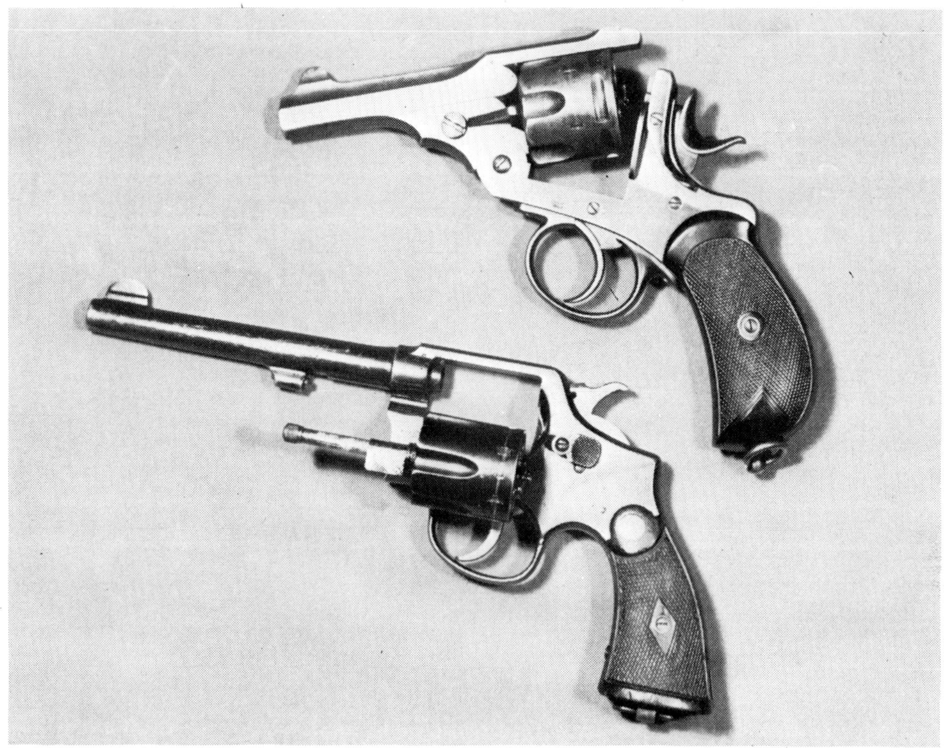

Top left: The .476 Enfield revolver first appeared in very small numbers in 1880 as the Mark I (*top*). The Mark II (*below*) was easier to manufacture but it still retained an interesting form of extraction in which the cartridge case rims were held by a semi-standing tree.

Left: In most early revolvers, as in this Adams (*top*), each cartridge case was separately extracted and ejected by a rod shown here pushed right through one chamber. When simultaneous extraction was attempted by hinging the frame some revolvers, as in this (*below*), had the hinge at the top.

Above: The simultaneous extraction and ejection of fired cases can be achieved by hinging the frame (Webley) or hinging the cylinder mount (Smith & Wesson and Colt).

sturdy arms American contemporary weapons do not really bear comparison. Not even the Colt Peacemaker of 1873 could really compete.

The centre-fire brass cartridge solved the basic problem but at the same time created others. Once fired, you had to get rid of it. In 1880 the British army adopted a .476 calibre revolver based on the design of Owen Jones, and Kaufman and Warnant. It had a hinged frame which extracted the fired cases by the motion of pulling the chamber forward whilst the cartridge cases were retained against the breech face by a tree engaged with their rims. In terms of improved efficiency this design, and its many variants, reached a stage further than their predecessor, the Adams, which had required the firer to knock out each fired case separately by means of a rod. This was a compound operation which obviously took far more time than simply opening a hinged frame. The revolver could work on the principle of being hinged at the bottom of the frame or, more rarely, at the top: it would alternatively achieve the same effect by a direct, straightforward pull of the barrel and cylinder, once unlocked, or it could use an underlever system to move the barrel and cylinder away from the standing breech face. But these are variations only of detail, however interesting such differences in mechanical operation may be to a collector today.

In the end it was the simple, forward, lower-hinge type, as used in the Webley family, which triumphed and went into British service. In America the form of case extraction which was finally adopted by Colt, Smith and Wesson and most other makers was one where the cylinder is swung out sideways, with the cases simultaneously extracted by manual movement rearwards of the centre axis, to which is attached a centre tree fitting under the cartridge rims.

The problems of high-speed extraction and ejection were solved, but loading each chamber separately remained a slow process. A solution came in the form of the Prideaux quick loader which, though patented in 1893, took some years to catch on. It worked well once it had been practised and it was probably marginally faster than changing cylinders, even compared with the Webley with the quick-release cylinder. This, incidentally, was a method of rapid reloading reasonably available to the user of a muzzle-loading revolver, but not really applicable to the breechloader where there was a high risk of spilling the cartridges.

The revolver relied upon the firer's physical effort for rotating the cylinder and cocking the hammer – utilising the recoil to eliminate this must have been a temptation. In 1895 and 1896 Colonel G. V. Fosbery, VC, designed the ultimate arm, the automatic revolver. Although it was not marketed on any scale until 1901 it was undoubtedly successful. In .455 calibre it achieved

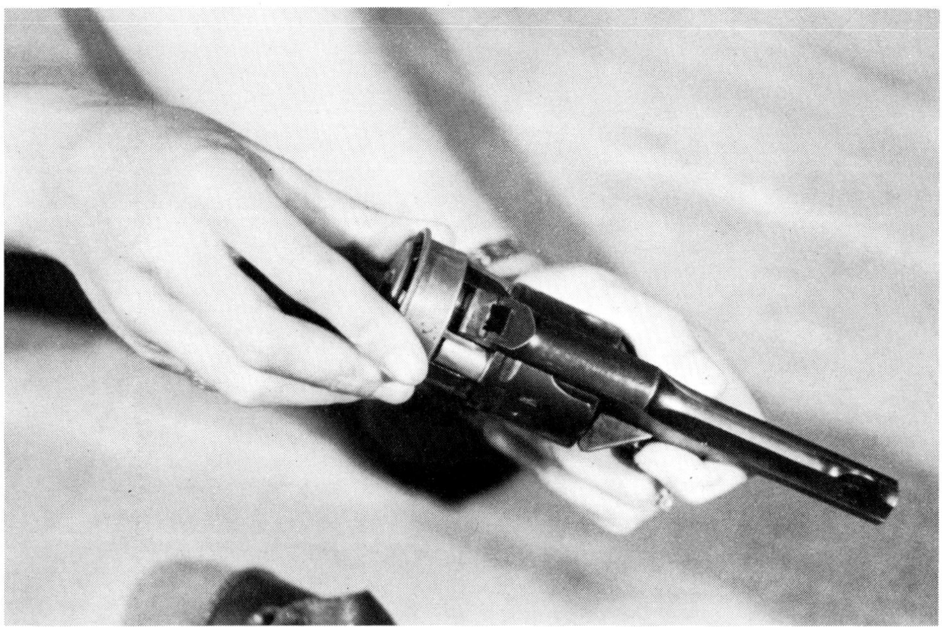

Rapid reloading of the Webley revolver could be achieved with Prideaux's quick loader which was carried ready for use in a special pouch in the belt.

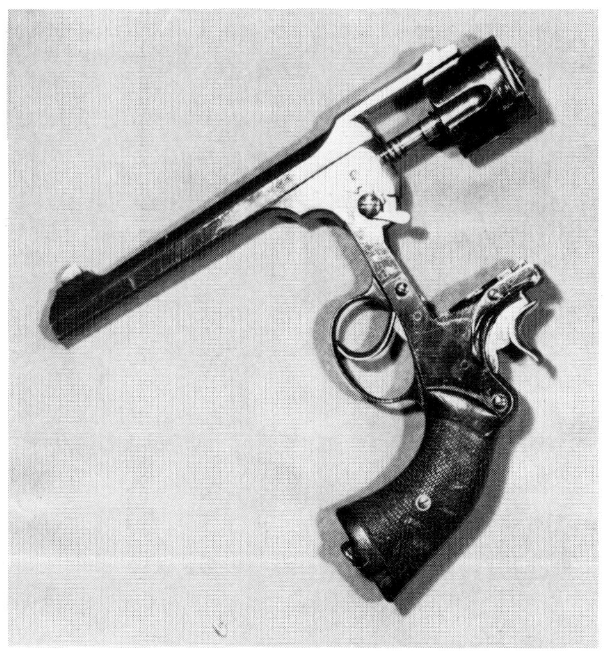

On the Webley WG revolver simple rotation of a small lever on the pivot pin permits the immediate removal of the cylinder and its replacement, if so wished, by a loaded one.

a considerable vogue in British service in the Great War. In .38 ACP, an eight-shot version really aimed at the American market, it was much less successful and is today a collector's item of considerable rarity.

When challenge to the revolver came, it was neither from the multi-barrelled pistol, nor even from the manually operated, mechanically self-loading pistol developed in the late nineteenth century – the so-called palm or squeezer pistols were the most common representatives of this class. It came from the automatic, or rather semi-automatic, pistol where the force of the explosion of one cartridge is harnessed to chamber and fire the next.

The earliest successful application of the principle of utilising recoil was Hiram Maxim's machine gun of 1884, but the first gas-operated machine gun was J. M. Browning's Colt design of 1890-5. In pistols the earliest successful self-loading design was the 8mm Schonberger of 1892, but, if it can claim priority in time, it is only by a short neck. By then others, including Bergman, were also designing comparable arms. Hugo Borchardt's pistol of 1893 was the first commercially successful model.

Who invented the semi-automatic pistol is really an academic matter. In real terms the semi-automatic military pistol hit the world stage in 1896 with the Mauser. So satisfactory was its design that it changed only in points of detail during the next fifty years. It was a gun good enough to be carried by the young Winston Churchill when all about him carried revolvers. It is curious that it should be a German-designed and made pistol which saved the life of the man who led us to victory over Germany. And yet more curious that, good though the semi-automatic pistol has become in the past eighty years, revolvers still command a substantial following.

6

Spearhead of Technology

Probably no two decades in history have seen such strides in arms development as the 1850s and 1860s. It is almost impossible to understand the revolution – for no weaker term would be appropriate – that lies behind the difference between, for example, the Pattern 1842 smooth-bore musket and the Martini Henry breechloading rifle. Even more amazing is the difference in performance between the India pattern flintlock Brown Bess musket of the Napoleonic Wars in the early nineteenth century and the Lee-Enfield rifle of the last decade of the century. With the former a man would only rarely be hit, when aimed at, from fifty yards, with the latter the same chance of being hit would be true for about 1000 yards.

The nineteenth century saw many changes: from the large-calibre smooth-bore musket to the small-bore rifle; the single-shot muzzleloader to the breechloading magazine rifle; the speed of the bullet at the muzzle rising from less than 1000 feet per second to well over 2000; the hand-made arm yielding to those mass-produced by machinery. But above all it saw death at 100 yards replaced by a similiar risk of death at nearly a mile. The effect upon battlefield tactics was profound but by no means immediate.

What was true for small arms was generally also true for ordnance. The links between the two fields were very close indeed. Many makers, such as Whitworth, Lancaster and Westley Richards, worked on the design of both ordnance and small arms. The Ordnance Select Committee, to whom almost all inventions with any sort of military potential were referred during the 1850s and 1860s, also covered the whole field. In spite of every effort to improve ordnance it was the rifle in the hands of the ordinary soldier which remained the key to the battlefield. And in this role it was also the key to national security through superior national defence. In spite of the physical, mental and economic effort which it took, many people and organisations patriotically designed and offered the perfect rifle to their country. This is

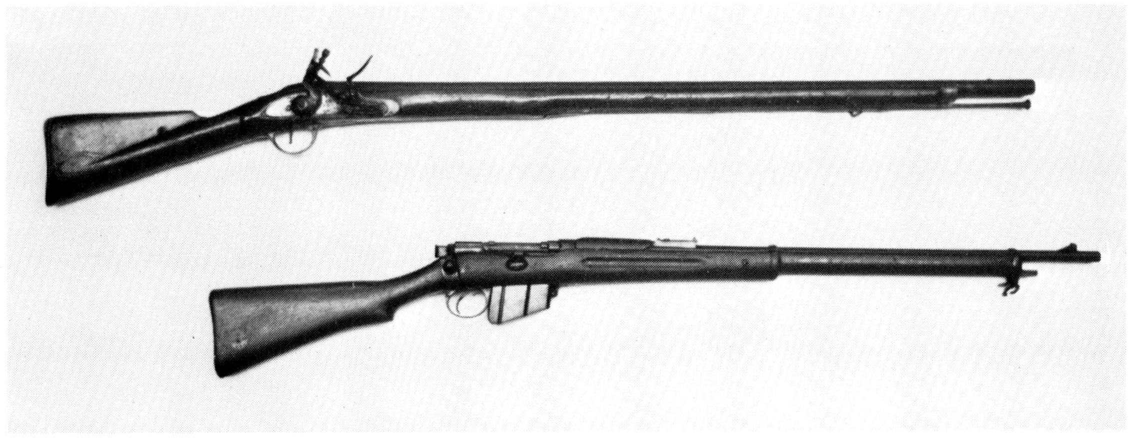

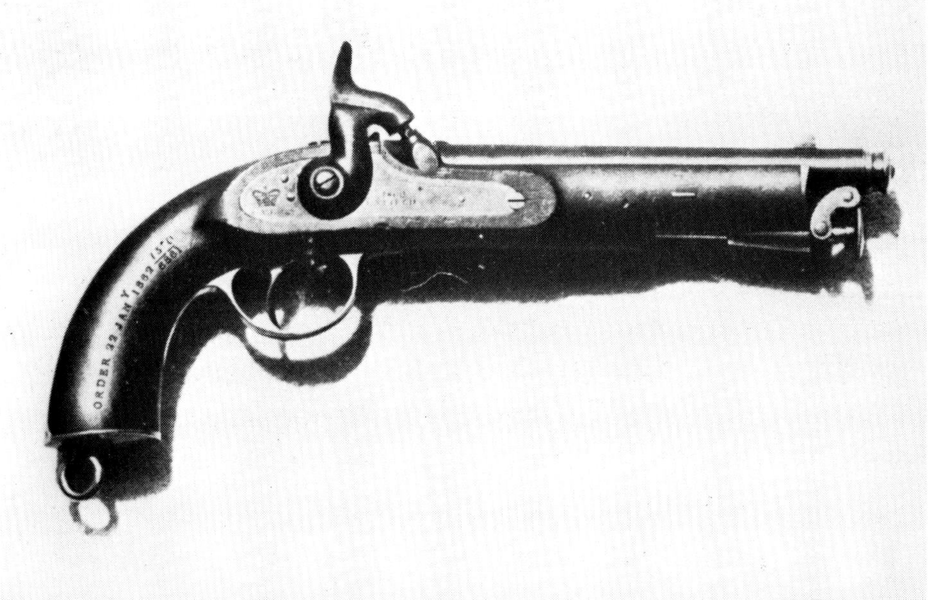

Top: The Brown Bess contrasted with the Lee Metford: an India Pattern smooth-bore, flintlock, muzzle-loading musket of the Napoleonic Wars compared with a .303 Lee Metford breechloading magazine rifle of the 1890s.

Bottom: From the 1860s photography began to be used as an alternative to holding a sealed pattern specimen.

clear from the records of the Ordnance Select Committee, and from contemporary newspapers and periodicals.

The mid-nineteenth century was a period of extensive, informed public debate about progress with the soldier's armoury. Many citizens, including some of the most eminent, having taken the immediate and obvious step of becoming volunteer riflemen, advocated major improvements in their armament. What was needed, so some of them very clearly saw, was a greater facility of supplying arms, greater range, greater durability, greater accuracy of fire and a greater rate of fire. Arguably the most important was the first, a greater supply of arms. In the early part of the nineteenth century when the only methods of manufacture were, as the word implies, by hand, the concept of turning out vast numbers of precisely-sized arms by machine seemed apparently unattainable. Not that no machines were in use: some simple ones were well established but they existed as extensions of hand-manufacturing processes rather than as part of machine production.

When war threatened, all that the Ordnance Department could do was to go out to the trade and attempt to contract for its increased requirements. But highly-skilled hand craftsmen were not easily enticed away from the routine, lucrative business of supplying the wealthy with fine firearms. The authorities had no option but to rely upon those who were not skilled enough to earn more money elsewhere. Not surprisingly, they found it extremely difficult to procure a sufficient quantity of satisfactory arms. There were a few makers who saw certain prestige in supplying the Ordnance Department with at least part of its needs. One of these was Henry Nock, who had a reputation second to none for workmanship and quality of design.

His reply to the Ordnance Department's extra requirements during the Napoleonic Wars was to organise his workshops so that the component parts of his arms were so precisely shaped and sized that they were interchangeable. In the event of breakage or damage on the battlefield, the affected components were easily replaced and the arm could immediately be used again. No longer would damaged arms be repairable only if a very competent gunsmith was available to file up suitable replacement parts. But Nock was not content in his remarkable achievement of interchangeability by hand rather than machine manufacture. He also redesigned the basic form of what we might term subassemblies. His screwless lock is a masterpiece of design. Its dismantling could not be simpler – even the inner lock plate could be removed by simply pressing a catch. He abolished the pan-spring, rationally making the mainspring do its work as well as powering the cock. There were no screws to lose and, though this was not the only screwless lock ever invented, it was probably the only one which got into quantity production. Curiously, one of

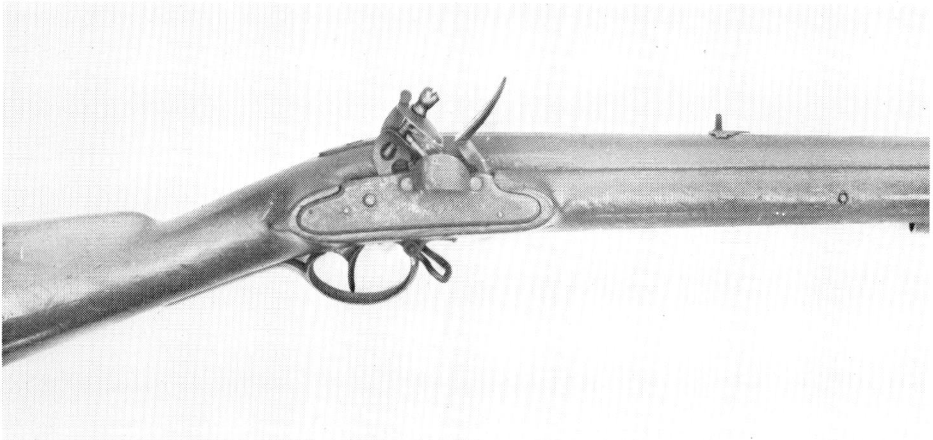

Top: Henry Nock's screwless flintlock with inner lock-plate removed. Note a single spring activates both the cock and the steel and pan cover.

Bottom: 'Baker' rifle by Henry Nock for Cambridge University Volunteers, fitted with his screwless flintlock, c. 1805.

Above: The sidewards escape of gas through the vent with a flintlock could be very considerable. The measure of recoil is apparent from the muzzle smoke being below the barrel axis.

Service rifles like this .22 Armalite can be assembled and brought into action within seconds of emerging from the water.

Most early telescope sights, such as this on Metford's 1865 2000-yard competition muzzle-loading match rifle, were very delicate.

Queen Victoria fires the first shot at the National Rifle Association's first meeting at Wimbledon, 1860.

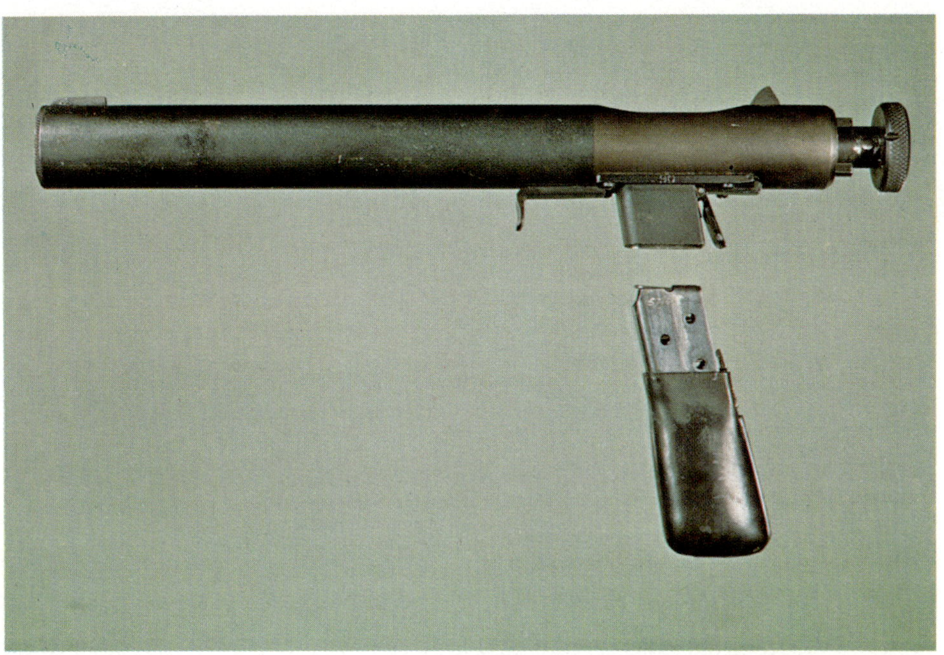

The silencing system in this Welrod pistol was efficient but only because, in spite of its 'automatic'-like appearance, it employed a locked breech and low-powered ammunition.

Few pistols have attracted more attention for their mechanical design that this Webley-Fosbery automatic revolver. Introduced in 1900 it eventually commanded a considerable following since it could be faulted only for its uncomfortably high line of sight.

Until the late 1850s the Royal Small Arms Factory at Enfield was very much a manufactory in the full sense of the word as this lock plate engraving reveals.

the very few other arms which also avoids the use of screws is the Mauser automatic pistol of 1896, in its later models.

The quality of Nock's locks – they were so well made that you could actually intermix the components of two different locks and both would still function perfectly – and of all his military arms was so high that new orders quickly followed. Then the problem came. Nock could not find extra gunsmiths of sufficient skill to increase his output and still maintain the perfection of manufacture essential for interchangeability. Those who were lucky enough to receive his arms clung to them ferociously: one regiment had them for thirty-two years, refusing all replacements normally due after twelve. Nock had discovered interchangeability but he had not sought a solution, and certainly did not offer one to the necessary means of mass production.

Credit for adapting machinery to the mass production of arms is usually given to Eli Whitney, the American inventor of the cotton gin. He first

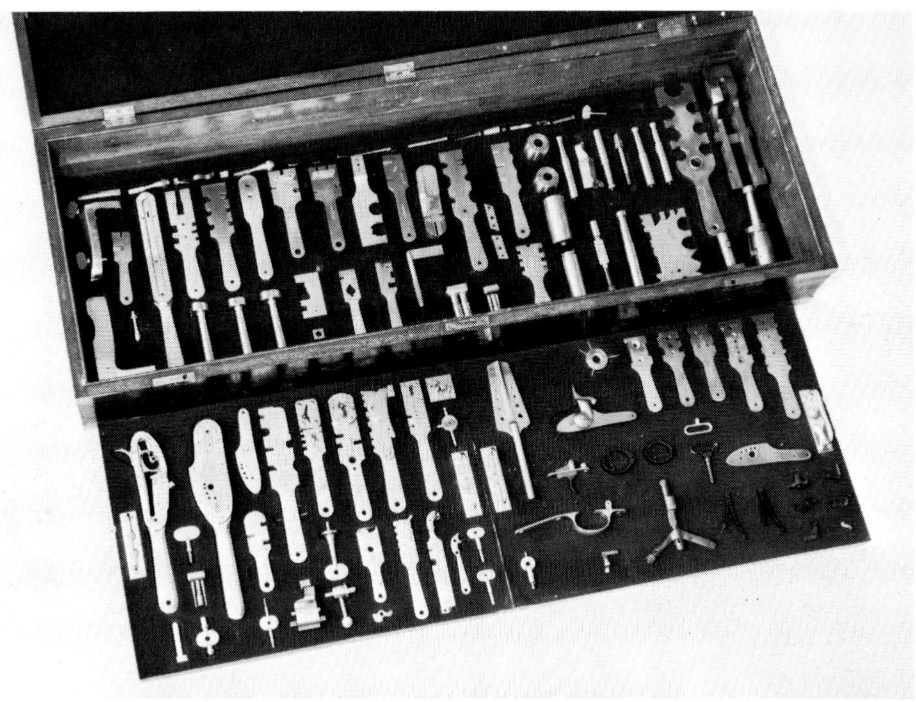

Probably no country controlled the quality of its manufacture of small arms as strictly as Britain in the 19th century. This set of gauges at the Royal Small Arms Factory, Enfield, covers every detail in the production of the Pattern '53 rifled musket.

contracted with Congress to supply arms in 1798. Between 1809 and 1824 it is calculated that he made 33,000 military flintlock muskets by machine. With Whitney's example the swing from hand to machine production slowly gathered momentum in the United States, but it did not really come to the notice of the British public until the Great Exhibition of 1851. Then it was largely through the revolvers of Colonel Samuel Colt.

During 1854 a British purchasing mission was sent to the United States to buy equipment for the new Royal Small Arms Factory at Enfield. It was so successful that some of the machines brought back were in use until well into the twentieth century. The Enfield factory, thus equipped in 1857-8, was quite a showplace, and provided a definite stimulus to others in the engineering or manufacturing world. The London Armoury Company adopted machine production techniques very early on. Finally, the Birmingham gunmakers, who thought of themselves as the centre of British arms manufacture, had no option but to organise themselves into the Birmingham Small Arms Company – BSA – a name probably better known today for motor bikes or some of its other products. But they had to find something to do to

Control of the precise pattern of arms was achieved in the 19th century by sealing pattern arms to guide manufacture. Such arms are today very rare and desirable collectors' items.

get through the lean years when the demand for guns throughout the world was low.

Once the principle of making all parts of the arm interchangeable by means of machine manufacture had been adopted, the problem of supply was nearly solved. At Enfield there was stringent quality control. Precise gauges ensured the true interchangeability of all components. For the first time the British Government could rest reasonably assured that, at the outbreak of war, it could obtain extra supplies of arms which were genuinely up to peacetime standard. The other requirements – range, durability, accuracy and rate of fire – largely depend on the actual design of the arm and that was by no means readily agreed. The Government would probably not have decided to set up the Enfield factory if they had not first assured themselves that a design could be devised that was suitable for mass production and up to their military requirements.

The man upon whom they chose to lean was Joseph Whitworth. By arms collectors Whitworth is remembered above all for his polygonal rifling, though it was not his invention and was never generally adopted in the army.

Whitworth's real contributions were to the science of accurate measurements, and to the standardisation of threads and gauges; his less direct but still crucial contribution was his general enthusiasm for the practicality of producing by machinery whole arms of the very highest standards as demanded by the British Ordnance authorities. Accuracy, standardisation and high quality were the hallmarks of all Whitworth's work. Some of his machines and tools have easily survived the century and a quarter since their manufacture. At Enfield they still use a Whitworth machine-rest for test-firing barrels.

The right intention and a benevolent environment were what Whitworth gave to arms development in the 1850s: the precise form of the improved machine-made rifle was the concern of the Ordnance Select Committee set up in 1855. It was their responsibility to advise the Government in everything military, ranging from the best mode of using balloons in warfare to the military applications of new forms of electric lighting. After 1856 the Committee was obliged by the Secretary of State to move towards leading rather than simply following design trends. In the field of small arms it was especially concerned with the fundamental requirement of adequate durability in the rifle. In a sense its task became easier as calibres became smaller – it was far more practical for a .45 Martini-Henry to have a barrel with reasonably thick strong walls than for similar strength to be achieved in a barrel of .577 calibre. However, to have increased the thickness of the barrel walls of the .303 Lee-Metford any further would have been to have favoured durability, and incidentally accuracy, to the detriment of other criteria. Barrels had to be thick enough not to get bent when a bayonet was misused and not to burst if accidentally partially blocked, but no thicker. The question of barrel strength was not really satisfactorily settled until steel was generally adopted in the middle of the 1860s.

It was not enough to aim simply at the durability of the barrel and action – the cartridge had to have adequate strength as well. The capping breechloader was never issued to the British army – in the form of the Montgomery Storm, it was actually adopted in 1864 – mainly because of the frailty of the skin of the intestine cartridge. Even when the Snider ousted the Montgomery Storm its rolled brass cartridge was still not the perfect solution. Solid brass cases were not really a practical proposition until about 1871: after that date the timing of their general adoption was purely a matter of balancing the economics of the move against the military advantages.

The goal of improved accuracy and range, which meant the best form of barrel and ammunition, was not one easily resolved by a committee like the Ordnance Select Committee in the mid 1850s. It consisted of ex-officio Heads of Departments, and although such high-ranking officials had the

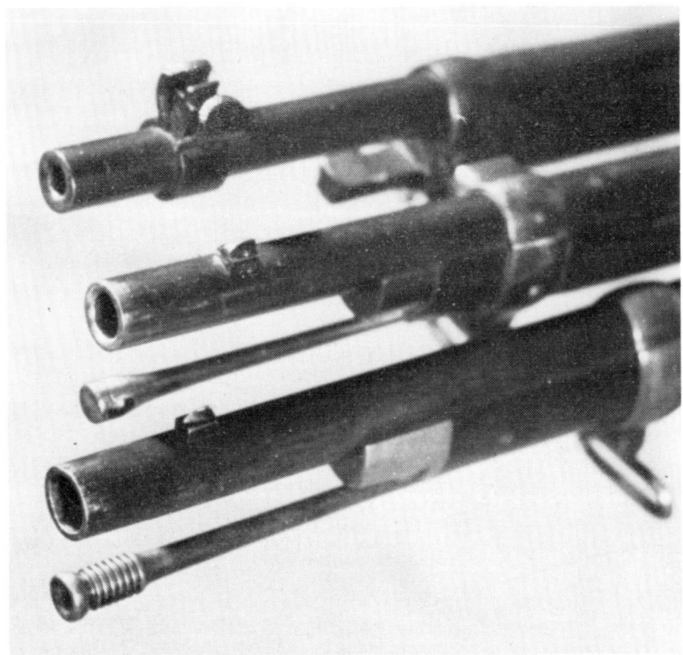

Top: As calibres decreased from the .577 (*bottom*) to the .45 and then to the .303 (*top*) so the barrel walls became proportionally and actually thicker, contributing appreciable accuracy of fire.

Bottom: Metford .461 paper-patched solid lead match rifle bullet (*top*) and a similar .45 bullet for the Martini-Henry breechloader.

It was William Metford's meticulous precision which contributed so much to the wide success of his rifles. This micrometer was his personal instrument; the notes accompanying it are in his hand.

power to keep things moving, they often had conflicting engagements which prevented their attendance and, regrettably, other interests and connections sometimes biased their judgement. In 1859 the Committee was reconstituted as a committee of full-time experts. It gained immensely in expertise, especially on detail, and, through a succession of first-rate presidents, General Lefroy in particular, it did not lose too much in prestige and influence.

The greatest contributions in the area of accuracy and range were made by private citizens. Under the Committee innumerable trials were held to determine the merits of the many designs of barrel and ammunition submitted. One particular man influenced the ideas that were submitted on this front. In his system, which became dominant in military as well as match small arms after 1870, the rifling consisted of very shallow-cut grooves which minimised friction between the walls of the bore and the paper-patched bullets of hardened lead. The bullet was so formed that it was only after expansion by firing that it acquired the optimum ballistic shape, and so sized too that, as it passed along the bore, the paper was just sufficiently incised that it dropped away from the bullet as it emerged at the muzzle. Had it not done so, accuracy would have been altogether lost.

The inventor of this clever and very successful system was William Ellis Metford, the same man who was responsible years earlier for the expanding bullet used in the P'53 rifled musket. Metford possessed mastery of detail as well as a concept of what the future would demand of firearms. In 1869-70, long before the Vickers Maxim arrived, he was worrying about accuracy of fire in the Montigny mitrailleuse. Others never got beyond a total preoccupation with the mechanism for loading and firing rapidly. Metford clearly foresaw that, as in most fields of development, success would eventually go to the most comprehensive weapon, coupled with a design which could be manufactured in quantity at reasonable cost.

The last criterion – greater rate of fire – is in a sense the theme of most of the chapters in this book. Important though the mechanism may be – and often the modern collector is aware of only this – it is definitely second to the barrel. First you had to hit your target then you had to try to do it as often as possible. Sheer firepower without accuracy can be awe-inspiring but it is not necessarily effective.

When the volunteers and their rifles first became commonplace in the mid-nineteenth century, countless citizens felt that they could contribute individually to the security of their country through the development and wider distribution of efficient arms. This development of arms was an all-consuming passion at the grass roots level and led to many of the great advances in technology, affecting the nation, and indeed society in general, even more widely than the actual advances in arms design.

Though to most people nothing can justify war except a threat to liberty, yet the general benefits arising out of a preoccupation with national defence flowed through the medium of technology into almost every aspect of Victorian life.

7

Riflemen All

It is a common mistake to believe that the development of the gun was a simple progression from the muzzle-loader to the breechloader. If a generalisation is permissible, the breechloader was first on the scene, but it was succeeded fairly early on by the muzzle-loader. That is the apparent picture, although in fact the breechloader had survived in specialist and esoteric firearms up to that time. In consequence, identifying the first modern breechloader to be used to a significant extent is a highly subjective exercise. To some La Chaumette's breechloader of the 1720s, which had a similar breech to the later Ferguson rifle, closed by a large, vertically-moving screw, might seem to be a candidate; others would plump for the Ferguson itself; but the majority would probably concede that not even Paully's breechloaders of 1810-20 really constituted a significant employment of breechloading in the military sense.

Most would still award the honour of the first significant military use of breechloading small arms to the Prussians. In the 1840s the limited introduction into Prussian service of a bolt-action needle rifle with cartridge loading – that is a rifle where a needle penetrates the cartridge case to detonate a priming element contained within it and within the powder charge – must be recognised as the opening of an epoch, even if that new age took some time to dawn. The British were sufficiently impressed to procure examples, copy them at Enfield and, in 1850, test them. They rejected the system as unsuitable for British military use because, unlike the Prussian, the British soldier had to be equipped ready to fight in the unspeakable cold of Canada or the incredible heat and humidity of India and Africa. The needle rifle, in their view, was not well suited to extreme climatic conditions. The French, on the other hand, did copy it. The famous Chassepôt, their principal arm in the Franco-Prussian War, was a needle rifle and performed well.

The main problem with any form of needle rifle was checking the escape of

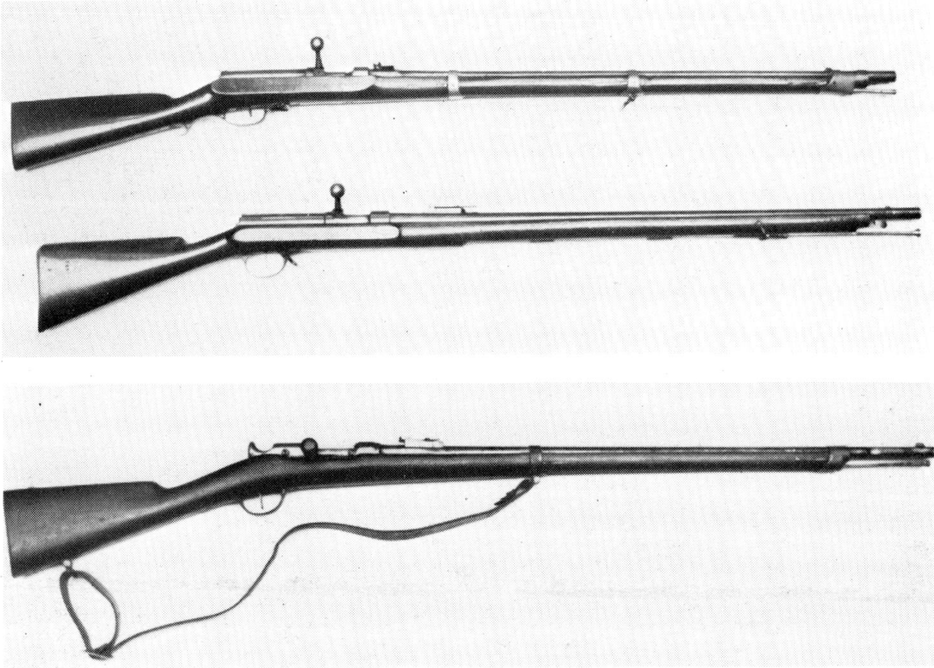

Top: The Prussian needle rifle model of 1842/49 (*above*) created such an impact in European military circles that the British decided to copy it and try it thoroughly. The Enfield needle rifle of 1850 (*below*) is an extremely rare arm as only six were made in the trials. The needle rifle was found wanting by British military standards.

Bottom: The French Chassepot model of 1866 was a highly refined version of the needle rifle, by most standards superior to that carried by the Prussians.

gas at the breech. There was a real danger not simply of a burnt thumb but even of blinding. In the Chassepôt the breech was sealed with a rubber obturator which expanded on firing to block the escape of gas. The rubber element needed fairly frequent replacement to remain effective, and the temper of the needle was decidedly affected by being in the heat of the exploding charge and had to be changed after about twenty shots. Before a second cartridge could be loaded there was usually a deposit of debris from the previous round to be removed.

The needle rifle enjoyed a certain military vogue on the Continent but is comparatively rarely encountered as a sporting system in England. We tended to pin our faith in the 1850s and 1860s upon the capping breechloader. In this the powder charge was in an intestine or skin envelope which was attached to the base of the bullet and the whole delicate assembly was protected until the

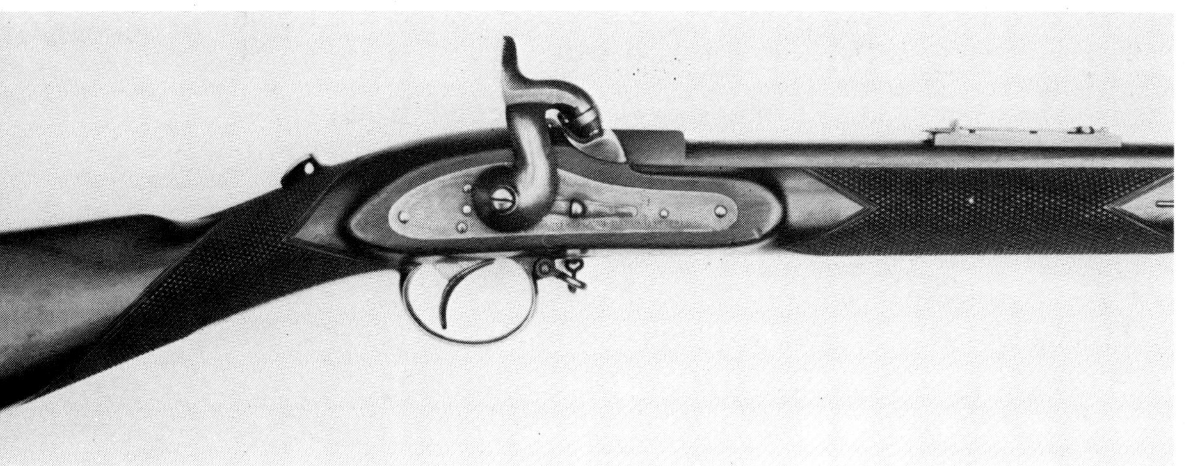

Top: .45 Westley Richards capping breechloader. In a similar form the Westley Richards was adopted by cavalry use and only just failed to be adopted by the infantry.

Bottom: Callisher and Terry's system of breechloading. Possibly unique as here applied to a pistol, c. 1855.

moment of loading by an outer paper jacket. Loading, therefore, consisted of pulling off the outer paper cover, pushing the cartridge, often with a felt wad attached to the end of the cylindrical powder envelope, into the chamber, closing the breech, capping the nipple, and finally cocking the mechanism. The flame from the exploding cap passed along the percussion communication or channel to penetrate the cartridge membrane. The breech in most of these arms was sealed by a brass obturator plug which momentarily expanded under the force of the explosion.

The capping breechloader's two major drawbacks were the fragility of its ammunition and the risks of severe gas escape at the breech. Exasperating at times though these defects could be, they did not stop the British cavalry trying a series of different systems. Perhaps the most famous were Sharp's, Callisher and Terry's, and Westley Richards's. Terry's system was adopted in 1858 for the cavalry's carbine whilst Westley Richards's, the most successful of all capping breechloaders, was so effective that in 1861 it was actually issued in rifle form to some infantry regiments for troop trials.

For a long time the British dabbled in breechloading. There was no great urgency in the matter, but with the 1860s the climate changed. Quite suddenly it was realised that we were in danger of being left behind by French, Prussian and other Continental armies in their move into breechloading. The quest was on in earnest to find not a new breechloader – that would have been far too expensive – but a cheap and efficient system of converting the enormous stocks of existing muzzle-loading P'53 rifled muskets into breechloaders. The result was the competition of 1864 and in November the Montgomery Storm capping breechloader was adopted for the armament of the army.

When an adequate supply of good-quality skin cartridges proved impossible to obtain, Colonel Boxer, Director of the Royal Laboratory, leapt into the breech instantly. His advice, which was eventually adopted, was to abandon the Storm and to adopt the American Snider because it used a durable cartridge, actually one of brass containing its own ignition – a cartridge to which Boxer made sure that his own name was firmly attached. In the Royal Laboratory the orphan boys were simply switched from rolling paper cartridge cases to rolling ones of brass foil on to which an iron base, carrying the cap, was riveted.

The Snider was very successful. The only trouble arose when the orphans – much cheaper than machines – accidentally left out one of the inner liners and the cartridge ruptured in the breech. Two remedies were eventually adopted: a small window in the outer coils to allow a visual check on the presence of the inner liner, and secondly, in the Mark III version, the action of the rifle itself was provided with a positively-locking catch on the breech block.

Replacing the Snider with a breechloader constructed as such *ab initio* proved very difficult. The struggle began in October 1866 with the announcement of a new competition. One hundred and four rifles were submitted: only nine were found to be seriously competitive. The nine designs entered stage two of the competition, with new rifles made closely to common standards including, logically, that of the barrel. All failed to reach the desired standard of accuracy, but the Henry took the prize for the best breech mechanism. At this stage the Martini was unsuccessful because its cartridges failed completely.

The Committee continued its enquiry by interviewing the leading figures in the field, from HRH The Duke of Cambridge downwards, to see what were most widely regarded as the desiderata in the ideal military breechloading rifle. Their chief decision was definitely to adopt .45 calibre.

In 1868 the competition was resumed to find the best barrel. Unfortunately for the country Metford, piqued by his earlier treatment by the authorities, refused to compete, so Alexander Henry was successful. The barrel's design settled, the trials once again turned to the question of the action. Sixty-five were tried competitively. The final ten designs divided into four bolt-action arms and six with blocks. A particularly severe test was applied to the bolt-action rifles to see if there was any danger of premature ignition of a faulty cartridge – those rounds with the cap left proud were particularly prone to accidents. Only one arm passed this test, the Carter and Edwards. Yet, in spite of its obvious excellence – its general lines were exceptionally neat, the action was adequately strong and would have later converted admirably to

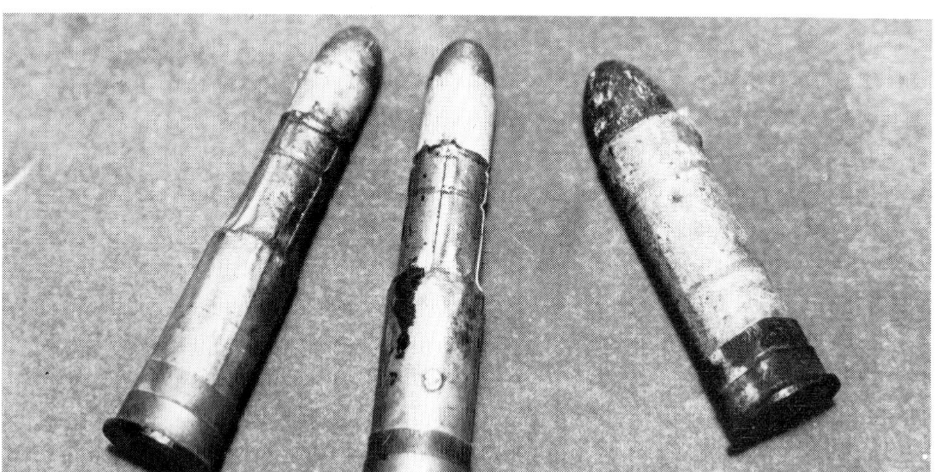

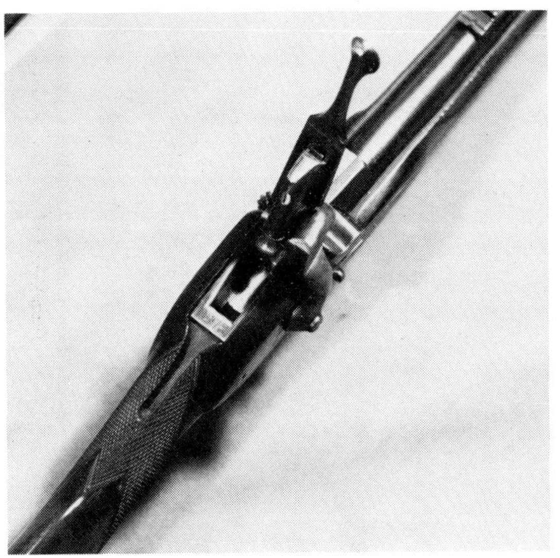

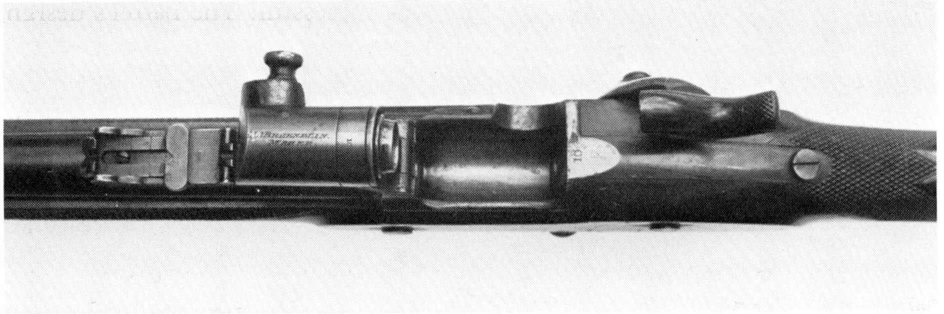

Above left: The comparative success of Westley Richards's capping breechloader owed much to a very efficient seal at the breech against escaping gas. The vital metal obturator can clearly be seen attached to a projection on the underside of the action lid.

Above right: After reports of the breech locks of Mark I and II Snider action (*right*) being blown open by defective cartridges a catch effecting a positive lock was introduced with the Mark III (*left*).

Bottom: The Montgomery Storm was officially adopted for the armament of the British Army, but an inability to procure a supply of adequate-quality skin cartridges led to its abandonment before issue.

Left: Two British .45 Martini-Henry coiled brass cartridge cases – one showing the inspection 'window' for a visual check on the round's completeness – and a .577 Snider coiled brass paper covered cartridge case.

Top: Carter and Edwards experimental military bolt-action breechloader.

Middle: Money and Walker's experimental military breechloader. Note the awkward high position of the breech opening and cocking lever.

Bottom: An experimental military breechloading rifle by Burton. One of hundreds of designs offered to the British Ordnance authorities in the late 1860s.

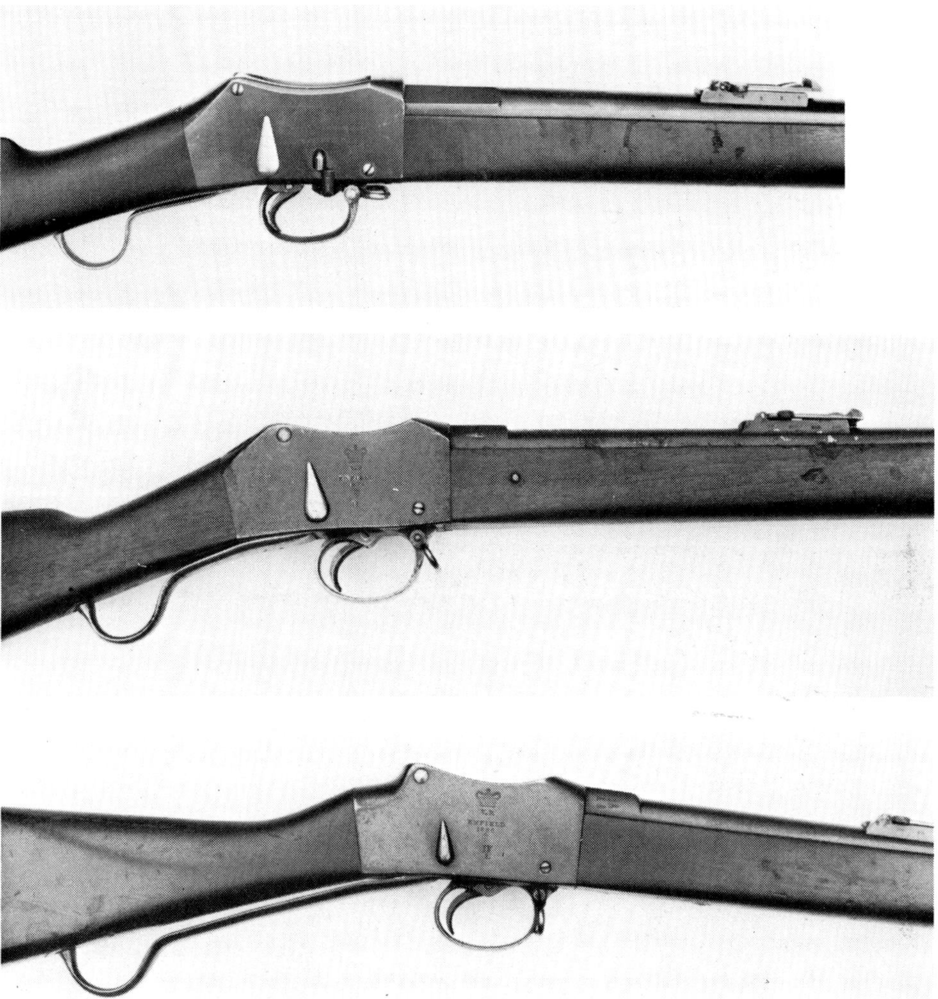

Top: Martini's breech action in a form very similar to that tested by the British authorities in the late 1860s. In a modified version it was later adopted.

Middle: .45 Martini-Henry Mk II.

Bottom: .45 Martini-Henry Mk IV Long Lever military breechloader. The Long Lever was an aid to difficult extraction of the fired cartridge case.

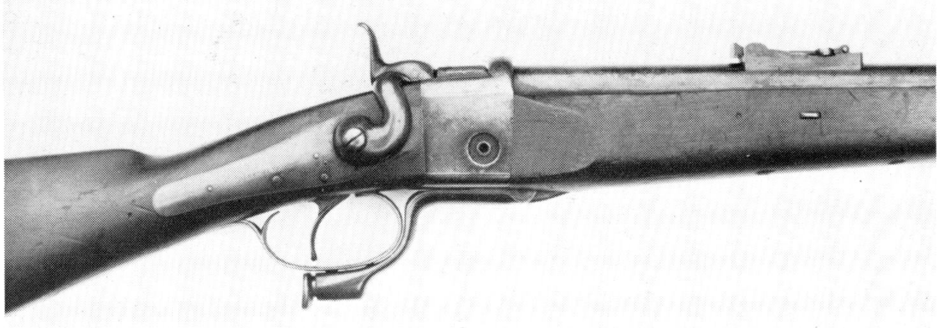

Top: .45 Henry military breechloading rifle c. 1868. Henry's breech action was narrowly beaten by Martini's so he had to be content with the adoption of his rifling system only.

Bottom: A falling-block centre-fire military breechloader by Westley Richards 1869. This was one of the Martini-Henry's most serious rivals.

magazine loading, and it functioned well – it was ruled out. The real reason was that Sir Henry Halford, one of the members of the Committee, had had his thumb very severely injured through a premature explosion in another bolt-action rifle. All bolt actions were therefore anathema. So the British army delayed by more than twenty years the means of introducing magazine loading. In Europe it was without doubt one of the most significant innovations of the last quarter of the century.

Of all the block actions examined by the Committee, the Soper, the fastest of all to operate, was not even seriously considered. Yet Private Warwick with a Soper rifle got off sixty rounds a minute in two formal trials, the one before the General Officer Commanding in Chief, the other before the Secretary of State for War. This is a rate of fire never matched by any magazine bolt-action rifle ever seen in British service. To the Committee the Soper seemed too complicated and that was the end of the matter as far as they were concerned.

Amongst the finalists with the Carter and Edwards were the Money and Walker, which was unpopular for its rather awkward lever action, and the Henry, a simple falling-block design activated by an underlever, which was runner-up to the Martini. In the end Henry had to be content that it was his design of barrel that was adopted. This was married to the Martini action, also one with a falling block and underlever, but instead of the external lock it had an internal striker activated by another novelty, a coiled spring.

The .45 Martini-Henry, formally adopted in 1869, was almost immediately under attack for its unmechanical design. The breech was opened and the cartridge extracted at just about the greatest mechanical disadvantage devisable! In Westley Richards's rival arms with similar external configuration the linkages were consciously devised to maximise the efficiency of extraction, ejection and cocking.

The opinions of the experts who fulminated against the Martini in its first few months of life were amply borne out by the experiences of those who carried them in action. In the Sudan especially its inadequacy was scandalous. When sand got in the action it became increasingly difficult to extract spent cartridges. Many a serious situation around Suakin and along the Nile was made yet more desperate by jammed Martinis. There was an official enquiry into the failure. In the final service pattern of this rifle, the Mark IV, a longer lever afforded some alleviation but there was very little that could be done to remedy such a fundamental deficiency, except to change from easily deformed, coiled brass to solid-drawn brass cartridge cases.

In America repeating rifles like the Winchester were quickly becoming fashionable, especially as the 1860s wore on. Such repeaters were rejected by the British authorities as underpowered – suitable only for short-distance warfare. One wonders whether the British soldier, with his shoulder smarting from the notorious kick of the Martini and its impressive bottle-necked cartridge, would have shared this view. In Europe by the 1870s centre-fire improved patterns of previously needle firearms for the moment seemed to predominate.

Logically, as was widely appreciated, the soldier would benefit most from the introduction of magazine loading. But with the dense smoke generated by black powder there was no great military advantage in speeding the rate of fire. Private Warwick with the Soper had vividly demonstrated this. The breakthrough came in 1886 when the French Lebel rifle became the first to use smokeless powder in combination with a smaller bore of only 8mm – naturally it was also magazine loading. With the introduction of the Lebel the genus of rifle which completely dominated the battlefield until the appearance of the machine gun had arrived.

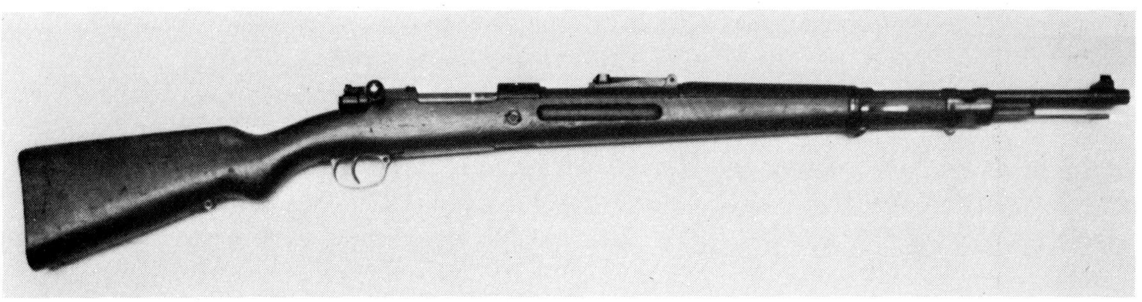

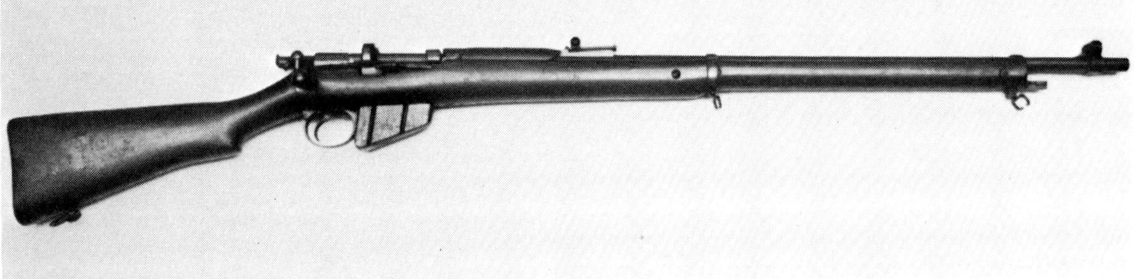

Top: German 7.9mm Mauser 1898/1924 service rifle. The Mauser '98 is one of the most famous of all military rifles and the long-standing rival of the Lee Enfield.

Bottom: .303 Long Lee Enfield service rifle with bridge charger guide, c. 1900.

Britain was still armed with the single-shot Martini-Henry: efforts to convert it to magazine loading were made but it was a challenge indeed. Even the best adaptations really belonged to the world of Heath Robinson. The Harston magazine loader worked quite well, but only when the soldier remembered to operate it muzzle down.

In the end it was realised that an entirely new design was essential. The one eventually adopted was the product of an American, James P. Lee of Ilion, New York. Metford was approached to lay down the specification for a small-bore barrel, not in .402 as earlier indications had suggested, but in .303. He did the job so well that it was adopted exactly to his formula and the rifle, as the Lee-Metford, began troop trials early in 1888.

At first in the Lee-Metford the British had to be content with a compressed black-powder cartridge imparting to the bullet rather less than 2000 feet per second muzzle velocity. But by November 1891 a smokeless cartridge loaded with cordite had been produced and manufactured. It certainly overcame the smoke problem but created another – barrel wear. The authorities decided to replace the shallow Metford rifled barrel with a new pattern with deeper rifling which, though Metford claimed it was also his design, led to a new designation for the rifle. So the celebrated Lee-Enfield had arrived.

The Boer War led to certain minor changes. Separate barrel lengths for the arms of the cavalry and the infantry vanished in favour of one standard. The resultant arm, which made its début in 1903, was called the Short, Magazine, Lee-Enfield or the SMLE.

The grass is always greener the other side of the fence, and it was only a few years later that the British were actively looking around for an improved rifle. The Mauser of 1898 attracted their attention. Theoretically it was an excellent rifle with all the most desirable features. The bolt was locked in place behind the cartridge by two large forward-positioned lugs, and there was a third lug towards the rear as a safety measure. Though there were other refinements, such as cocking on the opening movement, it was the forward-locking feature which was the great attraction since, unlike the Enfield, the accuracy of fire was scarcely affected by rain wetting the cartridges. In the end some experimental arms were produced – the pattern of 1913 – to a Mauser design and almost certainly would have been adopted had war been delayed. As it was, Britain entered the war largely equipped with the SMLE, though later large numbers of the P'14 Mauser-type rifles were procured from the States to supplement our supplies.

The Great War showed that things which are theoretically the best are not always best in practice. The SMLE was found to possess such a smooth action, even under muddy and difficult conditions, that a phenomenal rate of fire was attained by well-trained troops. Indeed, in the early stages of the war, it was this fact alone that led the Germans to conclude that the Old Contemptibles had many more machine guns than was actually the case. The SMLE proved itself the hard way to be a better rifle for the soldier than the Mauser 1898, P'14 or P'17, than the Mannlicher or Lebel, than the Ross or in fact any of the many rifles carried by the armies on either side.

While the early years of the War certainly mark the zenith of the rifle on the battlefield, this period also marks the beginning of the emergence of the machine gun as the queen of the battlefield. For there were two ways of achieving high fire power: either you had a good rifle in the hands of highly trained troops, or you had plenty of machine guns. The pace of the Great War was such that the expert riflemen of 1914 could not be replaced as they fell. And with their fall the rifle was forced to yield the supremacy of the battlefield.

8

Almost Beyond Price

A 'best English gun' is something almost sacred. No higher testimony could ever be asked than the effective head of Communist Russia confessing that there was no gift that he would treasure more than his own best English gun. In an age when England has yielded on almost every front since her days of universal hegemony, the 'best gun' is an unchanging feature in the landscape. Or is it so unchanging? Does hand-workmanship today mean what it did seventy years ago?

Outwardly, the best gun is superbly engraved, the height of hand-craftsmanship, yet in fact it conforms to a rigid stereotype. Few, if they were honest in their reply, would care to appear on the shooting field in England armed with a gun which does not 'conform'. Ideally they want to carry a double-barrelled, hammerless, sidelock ejector. There are never any sling swivels, which are exclusively reserved for rifles, and there is usually no butt plate. Engraving can be opulent in a discreet way, but never showy in a Continental or American fashion. Free from ostentation, it is perfectly English throughout and highly desirable. Paradoxically, it is built exactly to fit the client and yet it is intended to last for generations.

Not every English shotgun is produced to this stereotype, in fact quite the contrary. Apart from those intended for clay bird shooting in one or another of its competitive forms, there are the innumerable ordinary guns with which most of us have to be content. These days they are usually in 12 bore, 20 bore or .410 calibre, but there are many older black-powder-proof arms still surviving of other bore sizes, such as the 16 and 28 and, very rarely, the 24. Below these in size is a considerable family of saloon and garden guns, above them an ever diminishing array of wildfowling guns in ten, eight and even four bore. It is quite possible to find 'best guns' in most of these bore sizes, especially 16 and 20 bore, but usually the guns encountered will be of average quality; absolutely safe, assuming there is no serious danger of wear, but with

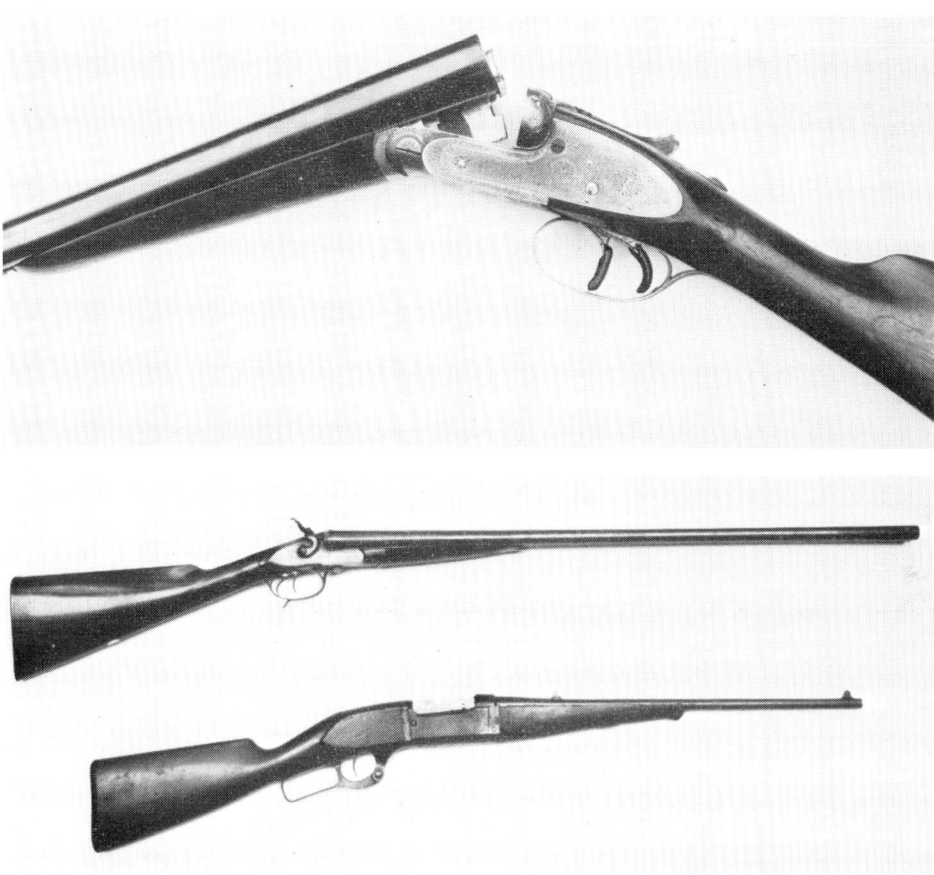

Top: Purdey 12 bore shotgun about 1895. In general lines typical of the vast majority of top quality English side lock shotguns.

Bottom: 16 bore double-barrelled, non-rebounding lock-hammer gun by Reilly, 1869 (*above*), and .22HP, model 1899, Savage sporting rifle.

boxlocks or hammer sidelocks and usually without ejectors or really fine engraving. Except for guns of pretty recent manufacture wood finishes will be oiled or polished – a modern plastic finish which is remotely as hard-wearing and pleasing to eye and hand still has to be invented.

The truth is that there was a gun for every purpose, from shooting sparrows at five yards to shooting geese at more than twelve times that distance. But that is not where the picture ends. It continues, in fact, to embrace the whole family of sporting rifles: a little confusing at times to the uninitiated since many double rifles resemble their gun counterparts very closely indeed. There

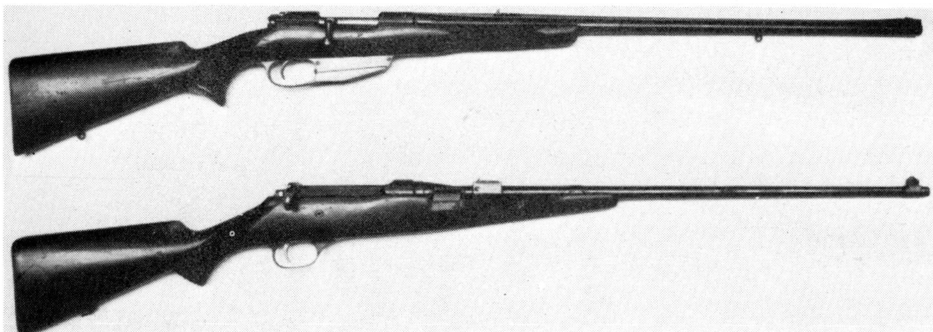

The Mannlicher bolt action was very popular in sporting rifles in the late 19th century and early 20th. This rifle *(top)* in .375 express was made by William Geener with a Mannlicher action. The Ross *(bottom)*, introduced in 1908, rapidly gained a considerable following in sporting circles. Its cartridge had a remarkable performance and, in the view of many, marks the beginning of modern, really high-velocity sporting arms.

are such rifles of the 'best' quality and with hammerless ejector actions. The give-away features are usually the weight of the barrels and their internal rifling, the frequent inclusion of sling swivels and of a pistol grip, and the almost invariable presence of sights. Occasionally a rifle is converted to a gun by boring out the barrels and removing the sights: it is a practice perhaps encountered most in the case of good-quality rook rifles. Such sporting rifles, and especially doubles, are still in the field of manufacture of 'best' arms, by the leading English makers. Within much less generous limits than your Edwardian predecessor you can still obtain the right gun or rifle for a particular task, whether it be a .577 3″ nitro express for elephant, a .375 nitro express for deer or an 8 bore for duck. There are only two provisos – that you can afford them and that you can afford to wait for them. For the 'best' guns and rifles are always in great demand and the process of producing a single arm can easily take up to a year.

The choice of wood for the stock is one of the earliest decisions a customer has to make. Nothing but the best walnut is used, with the final choice depending as much on beauty as on strength. Depending on the part of the tree used and where it was grown, the grain varies greatly. Once the customer's choice of walnut blank is established, the stockmaker has to transfer to the blank the guidelines of the precise measurements of cast off, bend and length – the client's exact measurements arising from his build, size and physical idiosyncrasies. The stock's ultimate shape is a now foregone conclusion, since only fully seasoned wood which is incapable of warping is used. It is possible, of course, for a blank to have a cavity or internal flaw: if so, another blank would be substituted. It is even possible to produce a completely satisfactory gun with a stock so shaped and dimensioned that a

Top: Damascus barrels as on this provincial 12 bore were not only light and strong, they were also extremely handsome. No steel barrel could offer comparable figuring.

Bottom: Although Nixon of Newark was, obviously, a provincial maker, the locks on this 1857 muzzle-loading percussion shotgun are very handsome examples of the engraver's skill and the choice of subject is typically apposite.

A shooting picnic, 1896.

man can fire from his right shoulder with his left eye – a 'cross-eyed' gun, in effect.

The action which the craftsman has to inlet into the stock blank so precisely is a product of a process relying much more upon hand than machine manufacture. However, there are some stages in its production when machines can save hours of painstaking filing without any loss of final individuality. None but an impractical purist would deny the logic of the balance most makers have struck between machine and hand work in both barrel and action. The external form of the action is still largely a matter of the smith's skill in wielding his chisel. Working with file and chisel, and with blacking lamp to check the running fit, the craftsman makes sure that metal and wood become as one and that the standing breeches have exactly the exterior form which is desired. The art lies in not removing the slightest bit more wood or steel than is necessary. It is easy to take away but almost impossible to put back.

The sidelocks themselves are masterpieces. Every component is separately finished and polished to a mirror surface. It is unimportant that they will be hidden from the eye behind the lock plate. Interestingly, their design has

The effects of the severe recoil of a heavy late Victorian big-game double rifle are clearly apparent.

M 1924 Belgian-made 1898 Mauser rifle (*above*), and .303 Enfield sporterised service rifle with telescope sight (*below*).

In the First World War the machine gun, and especially the Maxim, at last wrested the sovereignty of the battlefield from the rifle.

The magnificent quality of the walnut used in the manufacture at Enfield of British service firearms is exemplified in the stock of this .796 calibre Heavy Navy rifle of 1840. Near the butt trap can be seen the classification stamp 11CR (second class reserve).

hardly changed from that which became more or less standardised in the closing years of the last century, allowing each house its own special preferences. The secret of making a first-class lock is accurate, flat and square filing and fitting springs of the highest quality – there should be no perceptible loss of strength, even when left under compression for ten or twenty years at a time.

Today the manufacture of barrels is largely of outside provenance. However, at least one of the leading London makers, Holland and Holland, still makes its barrels, cutting them from solid steel and taking them the whole way through the manufacturing process on their premises. The customer's choice is now limited to steel barrels. There is no question about their strength but there is no doubt either that in terms of beauty they stand second to the finest Damascus. Unfortunately there is no one alive with the expertise to make a Damascus barrel. The individual bars were built up from horse-shoe nails and other special sources, and according to the precise structure and metallic composition of the iron and steel so the final twist or Damascus barrels acquired one of a wide range of particular figurings and colour contrasts.

Though less dramatic, the process of producing steel barrels is still totally dependent upon the handcraft of the barrel-maker. The eye alone is used to check the precise straightening of the bore by a method known as sighting. This is simply a matter of using the shadow of a window-bar falling along the interior of the bore as a means of revealing and locating any deviation from absolute trueness. Any aberration is removed either by tapping the barrel with a hammer or pressing it in a hand-press.

A double gun is, in effect, two single-barrelled shotguns, but joining them so that they shoot together is, and always was, one of the areas where the barrel-maker's skill is at its peak. After they have been brought into the required juxtaposition by wiring, the barrel-maker, taking his time and using a slow furnace to avoid hardening the metal, carefully brazes them together. Once joined, two ribs are attached either side by tinning so that the barrels acquire the appearance of being a single entity. It looks a straightforward operation but, as a nineteenth-century gunsmith warned, 'the whole of the space between the ribs and the barrels must be completely filled with solder or rust will form there with serious consequences'.

The process of making double barrels calls for fine judgement and great expertise. Though the same nineteenth-century gunsmith wrote that 'it is very doubtful if any two gunsmiths will agree as to the inclination of a pair of barrels' – meaning their precise juxtaposition before joining – they still had to shoot together. However, it was not left totally to the eye of the barrel-maker.

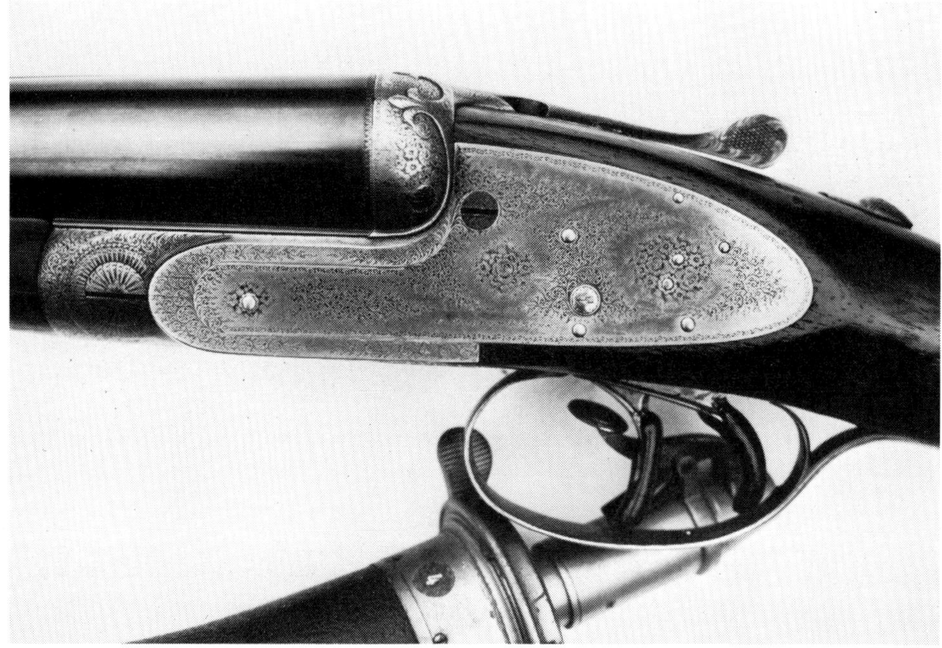

The leading English shotgun makers each had their own house style in engraving. Purdey's is so well known as to be quite unmistakable.

The gun was assembled and shot on the range, usually at forty yards. A given percentage of pellets have to strike inside a 30-inch circle. An unchoked barrel with a given cartridge of 234 pellets had to put 50% of them within the circle whereas a fully choked barrel had to reach 70%. The distribution of the pellets obviously had to be fairly even – an irregular pattern through which a bird could fly unscathed was unacceptable.

If the patterning showed that one or both barrels needed further attention then the gunsmith returned to lapping the bores, but he had to be careful not to remove so much metal that the interior dimensions were taken out of tolerance. A 12 bore, which was a gun with a bore of the diameter of a pure lead ball weighing one twelfth of a pound, is now standardised as .729″. So the smith had to aim to achieve the desired correction without going out of tolerance, and without in any way impairing the mirror finish of the interior of the bores. This was not too difficult as his attention would be directed mainly to adjusting the constriction towards the end of the muzzle, the choke, which concentrates the shot as it leaves the barrel.

Equally, the finishing stages, through which the gun or rifle must pass, have changed little in the last century. The stock is chequered, which is

Engraving on fine-quality shotguns is often suitably appropriate to their intended usage, as the duck on the lock plate of this 10 bore muzzle-loader.

functional in that it ensures that the hand does not slip, and decorative in that it is the last remnant of the earlier fashion of carving the stock. Then it requires finishing. The secret of the incomparable appearance of the walnut of a best gun lies in a combination of linseed oiling, sanding, pumicing and re-oiling, day after day, week after week, sometimes for a year or more. There is no short cut. But the final result is not simply a joy to behold, it perfectly ensures the preservation of the wood.

The action body, the lock plates and furniture are passed to the engraver for the penultimate stage in their finishing. There is almost no limit to the choice of subject: the engraver's artistic flair and cutting skill can cope with almost anything. For clients who have no definite views there are pattern books from which to make their choice; and for those who want something stamped with their own individuality or, perhaps, their special hero – Napoleon, for example – then that can also be delivered. The engraver's freedom is not quite complete: there are the obvious limitations of the format; wherever possible he seeks to use his work to take the eye away from joints and pin heads; and he might be reluctant to engrave a gun in a style closely associated with another firm. However, it is somewhat invidious that he alone signs the gun, when almost all those responsible for creating it are also artists and craftsmen in their own right.

With the engravings complete, normally the metalwork is finally blued by case-hardening. There are other methods, including the use of cold chemical solutions, but they usually lack the deep lustre of blueing by case-hardening. To some no blueing can compare with browning, once the only fashionably acceptable finish, but today it is distinctly out of favour.

Finally the gun emerges finished, an elegant and totally alluring amalgam of blued and engraved steel, set in polished walnut of the richest hue and spectacular figuring – a work of art by the standards of any age. Yet, behind the sumptuous façade, lies a thoroughly efficient, complex, and perfectly finished mechanism. The whole is the ideal instrument for its purpose, and the culmination of months of craftsmanship from a team of men. In spite of the long apprenticeship inseparable from the attainment of such skill, in spite of the apparent competition from machine-made mass-produced arms and in spite of the considerable expense of the raw materials the 'best' English gun of the late twentieth century is a worthy successor to its long line of predecessors, and there are plenty of customers willing to pay heavily for the privilege of ownership.

Today, even the plainest of the 'best' guns can cost thousands of pounds. Those which come from the upper end of the bracket, in terms of the magnificence of their wood and elaboration of their decoration, can cost tens of thousands. Recently clients of one London firm competed for the right to pay £26,500 for a double-barelled .600 nitro express elephant rifle!

9

Accurate at a Mile

In 1888 Sir Henry Halford, the Captain of the English Eight, exhorted the country gentlemen of England to take up high-class rifle shooting both as a sport and as a business. Today the term 'gentlemen' may be a trifle elastic but match rifle shooting is still the most exclusive form of the art and probably the only one which is peculiarly British.

For those who want to try the pleasures of attempting to hit a bull's-eye only two feet in diameter at distances of more than 900 yards there are facilities at Bisley and membership of the English VIII Club or the National Rifle Club of Scotland is open on application. The Cambridge University Long Range Rifle Club, founded in 1864, exists for those steeped in match rifle shooting, and especially for those who were formerly shots at Oxford and Cambridge.

Match rifle shooting is the supreme test of wind judgement and the interpretation of atmospheric and other data. It is an exact and scientific sport. Even staying on a target only ten feet wide and six feet high can be a very challenging task at 1200 yards. A constant watch has to be kept on wind speed and direction, never easily read off the flags and often difficult to determine from the mirage. Having decided upon the wind factor, the firer has to apply it to the vernier scales on his sights and take his shot before conditions change.

Temperature is another critical factor. At 1000 yards, for every 10°F the firer must correct his aim, or adjust his sights, by about a foot on the target. Barometric changes must also be noted, and at distances beyond 1200 yards even such factors as the rotation of the earth and drift imparted by the direction of the rifling must be taken into account.

The variety of types of rifle, the personal differences in position and the wide range of sighting systems all testify to a sport which has almost limitless scope for individual inventiveness. So long as the barrel does not exceed a certain weight, the same cartridge batch is used and the rifle is not directly rested at its fore-end on the ground, one wins or loses very much in proportion

Sir Henry Halford, Captain of the English Eight and a prominent shot at Wimbledon from 1862 onwards. He collaborated with William Metford for over 30 years, until the healths of both broke in the mid-1890s.

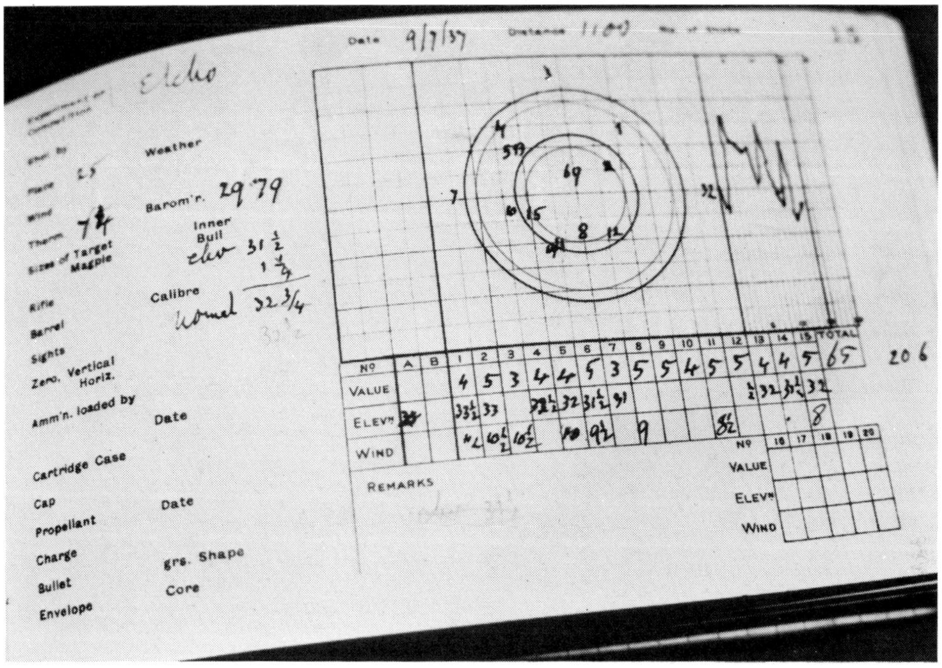

In most forms of shooting wind and weather conditions matter greatly. Score books have been used to record vital data for at least 115 years.

to what one puts into the sport in effort, developing expertise and, above all, in care. The Cambridge Club can be seen as a microcosm of the wider field of target shooting, with members ranging in age from eighteen to eighty. Perhaps it is not so typical of the broader scene as members still pay the same subscription as that fixed in 1862, only £2. Nor is it typical, indeed it is unique, in the survival of Victorian range etiquette at its annual prize meeting. One custom is that each individual shot is called and each firer warned of his turn to fire. This is not a pointless procedure with six or seven firers on each target often waiting at least five minutes between successive shots. It's easy to fall asleep in the warmth of a June day.

It is a tiring and demanding course of fire which extends over two whole days – so demanding in its attenuated form that it has been described as a course of ninety sighting shots. Yet, over the years, many pioneers of arms design as well as the foremost rifle shots in the land have come to Cambridge to compete. Sir Henry Halford, William Metford and the late Lord Cottesloe are but three who have competed for the Cambridge Cup. Members have come to Cambridge, met together and since the 1880s dined in Selwyn College, and the Cup which goes to the best shot has become one of the premier shooting awards in the land.

An English Eight in the 1880s, with their fine .461 back-position breechloaders.

The Crescent City (New Orleans) Rifle Team photographed at the time of the international match, 1877.

In 1862 Lord Wemyss gave the Elcho Shield for competition between England, Scotland and Ireland. Today the annual match continues, with a record book of past matches which is a mine of information on rifles, ammunition and individual performance. But keen though competition was between the home countries, the great question was always whether we were better shots than the Americans.

In 1873 when the Irish won the Elcho Shield for the first time, and with a very good score too, they sent a challenge to the Amateur Rifle Club of New York. The Americans, though new to shooting at 800, 900 and 1000 yards – the conditions were as for the Elcho – still beat the Irish by three points. One of the Irish put a bull on the wrong target!

That was the first in a series of matches between the English, Irish and Americans which were a great stimulus to the development of the match rifle. Perhaps the most famous was the 1876 match which the Americans won again, beating the Irish, Australians, Scots and Canadians. In 1880 the British finally had their revenge when a team captained by Sir Henry Halford triumphed at Wimbledon. They consolidated their victory with further successes in 1881 and 1882. But sadly, that was the end of the series. These matches were major social occasions, had been watched by enormous crowds, and great numbers of newspaper column inches were devoted to recording every facet of them.

They had demonstrated simultaneously that the Metford system was the most accurate available and that the breechloader had a decisive edge over the muzzle-loader. At least that was the only conclusion possible by the early 1880s. In the form of the Gibbs Metford Farquharson, a .461 breechloader with falling block, there was little room for further development whilst black powder remained the propellant. The highest-quality black powder shot very well but in dry weather was best if its fouling were kept in a fairly mastic condition by the firer blowing down the barrel after each shot. Certainly it had to be stored away from all moisture too. Not surprisingly match riflemen stuck to their .461 breechloaders for eight years after the army had adopted the .303 small bore. Scores such as those made by Major Lamb in 1892 on the 36″ bullseye of 219 ex 225 at 800, 900 and 1000 yards could not be denied, and so the small bore did not oust the .461 match rifle until 1897.

Scores naturally slumped but soon picked up. The Lee-Metford acquitted itself very well as a match rifle as well as a service rifle. In 1904 seven out of the winning English VIII used it with special sights, though the ammunition was still loaded with round-nosed bullets. But there was always room for improvement. In 1908 Sir Charles Ross introduced a new rifle with multi-lugged bolt and optical foresight and a new cartridge with a long pointed

The international rifle matches of the 1870s and early 1880s were very popular occasions both sides of the Atlantic. Part of the crowd at Creedmoor, 1877.

bullet. The cartridge was .303/.375 and proved very accurate, leading almost directly to the introduction in 1912 of a 'central', an innermost scoring ring, inside the bull's-eye.

For most of this century Mannlichers and Mausers have dominated the scene. The picture began to change only in the early 1960s. In 1964 the .303 streamline cartridge was replaced by the 7.62 mm NATO cartridge, albeit with a heavier bullet than in ordinary service usage, and many competitors turned to new actions to convert. Some went to the specially made heavy Schultz and Larsen but, particularly after the change of calibre in service rifle class (b), now known as target rifle, others converted the Lee-Enfield. The same No. 4 rifle which was the principal arm of the British forces throughout the Second World War and which was the direct descendant of the No. 1 or SMLE rifle of the First World War, became used increasingly for match rifles. One of these No. 4 Enfield match rifles has recently achieved the remarkable feat of winning the Hopton Medal, the Match Rifle Championship of the Imperial Meeting at Bisley, three times in four years. Yet in theory the Enfield action is all wrong. It is rear-locking and very easily affected by rain. A wet

This use of the telephone for communication between the butts and firing point in America in 1877 must be a pioneer in this field.

cartridge case binds less efficiently to the chamber walls and so transmits a much greater load to the bolt face which, compressing in its own length, allows the bullet to leave the muzzle at a different point on the barrel's flip. As the Enfield is rather light it is therefore of none too stable construction.

Not surprisingly, the remarkable recent success of the No. 4 Lee-Enfield rifle in the Hopton Medal was matched by its successes in the Queen's Prize, the summit of the year's shooting for all marksmen in the Commonwealth. Unlike the placid calm of the match rifle field at Cambridge, or even at Bisley, the Queen's Prize for 7.62 mm target rifles is a bustling and intense occasion. The test is one of rifle, eyesight, physique and, above all, nerve. A celebrated match rifleman of the 1860s, Captain Heaton, gave the following advice, which is as true today as it was then: 'Should you make a bad shot at the commencement of the match, you should never lose heart: you should rather remember that finishing well after starting badly is a very satisfactory way of winning the prize.'

A target rifle is one of military bolt action or similar design which was or is in quantity production and which is fitted with a barrel weighing not more than $4\frac{1}{2}$ lbs. Thus target rifle shooting in general, and the Queen's Prize in particular, sees direct and vigorous competition between Mausers, Mannlichers, Schmidt Rubins, P '14s, Lee-Enfields and many others. Every year the message is the same. In spite of all the effort put into finding a better rifle the No. 4 Enfield remains incomparably the best rifle action for the target marksmen. In 1976 the Queen's Prize went to an Enfield yet again, a rifle almost indentical in every significant mechanical feature with that first adopted by the British army in 1888. What greater triumph of empiricism over theory could there be? Nor what closer link between the two great fraternities of full-bore marksmen, the TR and MR shots.

.461 Gibbs Metford Farquharson breechloading match rifle.

.303 Long Lee Enfield with special pistol grip and optical foresight, first permitted in 1905 (*extreme left front row*).

Lord Cottesloe's rifle, with which he had just won the Cambridge Cup, is fitted with a long telescope sight, offset to the left and positioned for back-position shooting.

These photographs (*above* and on *opposite page*), taken at a shoot of the Cambridge University Long Range Rifle Club at Grange Road, Cambridge in the 1890s, clearly show the whole operation of shooting with the long range match rifle. Note particularly that one firer is either setting his foresight windage or blowing down the bore to loosen black powder fouling, whilst, behind the firers, scorers with large telescopes on tripods record on the miniature targets beside them the location of the firers' shots.

It was here that the Metford rifle made its triumphant début in 1865. Sir Henry Halford, who won the Cambridge Cup in that year, with this rifle, recognised the epoch-making character of the event by carrying a section cut from the barrel on his watch chain for the rest of his life. A fitting gesture because this rifle was so successful that it entirely dominated both the military and the match rifle scene for almost the whole of the rest of the century. Although Sir Henry used a muzzle-loader, Metford's barrel in breechloaders was even more successful.

It was also in 1865 that Metford won the National Rifle Association 2000 yards' competition – a remarkable distance at that date. The rifle with a special heavy barrel was designed to be shot in the back position with a telescopic sight. It is therefore interesting on two counts, both as an early example of an English rifle designed to be shot in the supine position and in using a telescopic sight in this configuration. The supine position has the advantage of permitting the direct transfer of the weight of the rifle, through the bone contacts of knee and ankle, to the ground. Provided that the actual position assumed is rather more on the side than the back proper, there is little strain upon the neck muscles. There are variants of the back position, including one called the 'peerage' position, where the other leg is laid flat rather than pointing upwards bent at the knee. Most of those positions seen depicted in nineteenth-century coloured prints are apocryphal! Shooting in the prone position, which remained the norm in match rifle throughout the 1860s and 1870s, had the drawback of causing some people severe backache, when a long period was spent on the point.

However, it was American success with the back postion, rather than any glaring defect of the prone position, which led to its gradual adoption in England in the 1870s. Muzzle-loading match rifles normally have their backsight positioned on the small of the butt. It is possible to shoot rifles of this configuration either in the prone or supine position but for a comfortable back position the sight eventually was moved to the heel of the butt. Only very rarely will a muzzle-loading match rifle be found with its backsight in this position, but it became common with the introduction of breechloading. In 1878, during the transition of muzzle- to breechloading and prone to supine shooting, an enterprising Scottish gunmaker, Alexander Henry, patented a dual-position rifle with two triggers and pistol grips and, in effect, two butt plates. It is a great rarity today but examples of Henry's rifle are known in both muzzle- and breechloading form. By the 1890s almost everyone shot in the supine position and so it remained until well into this

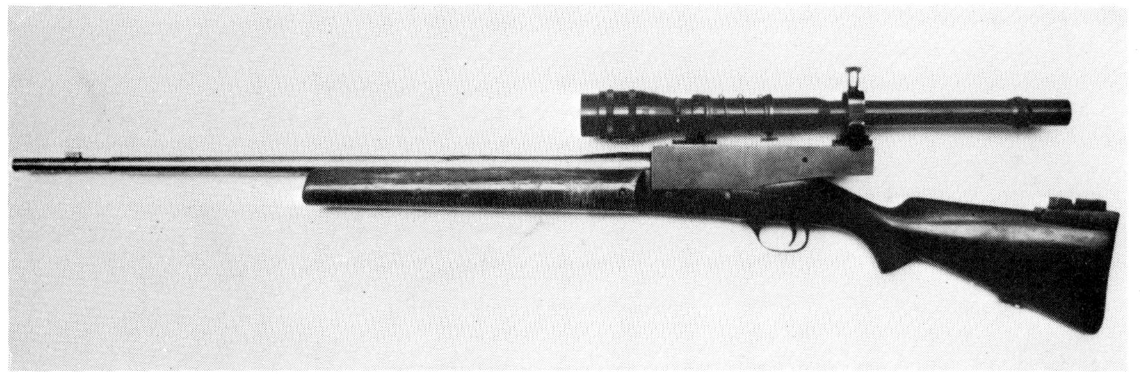

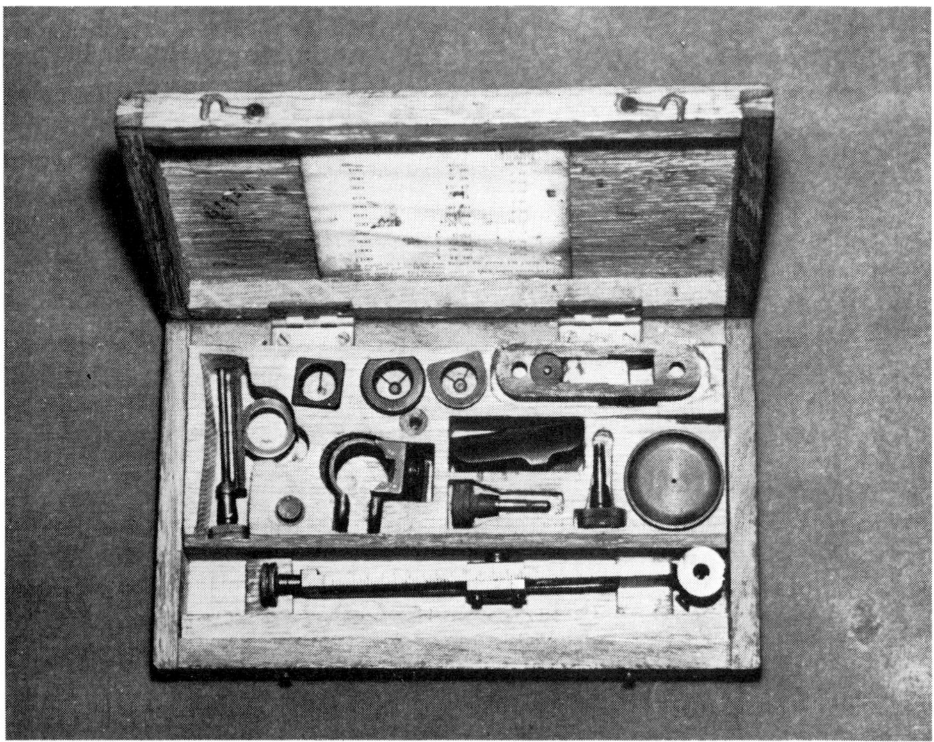

Top: Telescope sights are normally mounted on match rifles for use in the prone position, but very occasionally they are fitted for supine shooting as with this Bausch & Lomb 6-24-power on a Ross, model 1905, rifle.

Bottom: A set of match rifles special supine position sights for fixing to a military breech loader for match shooting, c. 1895.

.303 P'14 Enfield Service rifle which saw extensive service in both World Wars and is today one of the mainstays of target rifle shooting in the UK.

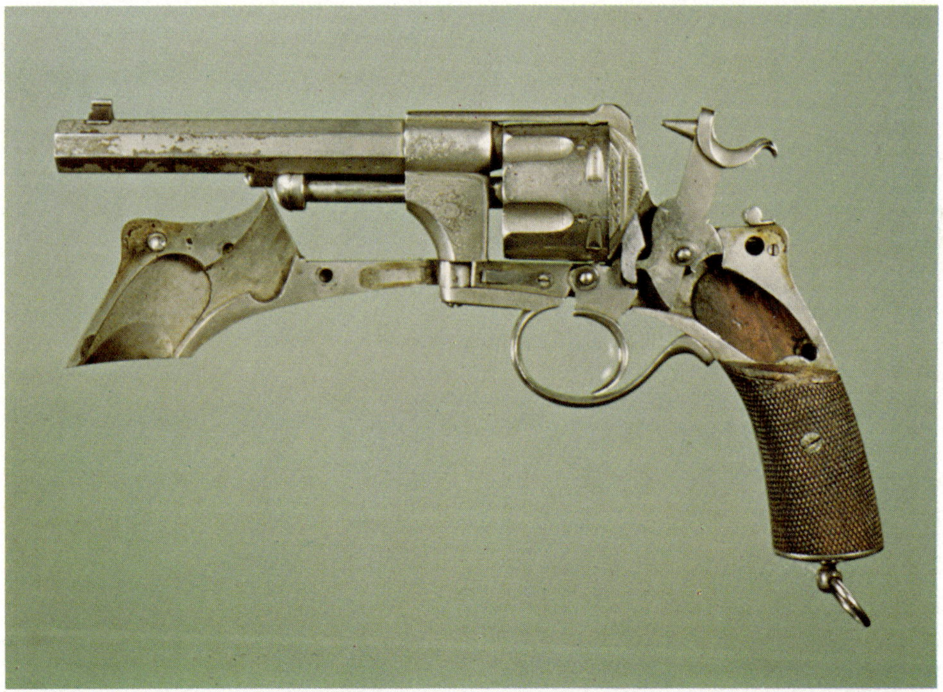

There were two schools of thought on the best way of achieving reliable performance under battlefield conditions. Either the mechanism was virtually sealed off and the soldier hoped sand and dirt would not penetrate to jam the action or, as in this Gasser revolver, a hinged plate or similar feature gave immediate access for thorough and rapid cleaning.

.303 Lee Enfield Jungle carbine.

.303 Lee Enfield No. 4 rifle with service 'scope for sniping.

century. Even today, and in spite of the claims of prone shots to be able to see the wind right up to the moment of firing – something you cannot do if the wind is from the left and you fire in the back position with the left knee up – about half those shooting match rifle still favour the supine position.

The telescope with which Metford's 1865 2000 yards rifle was fitted stood in sharp distinction to the iron sights of contemporary match rifles. Although by using sights of great delicacy, with Verniers engraved on platinum, taking a range of interchangeable sighting elements, and almost always with aperture backsights, they were capable of all the accuracy in aiming ever required, they were still of iron construction and thus susceptible to adverse weather conditions. It was not until 1905 that optical sights were permitted in competition. Then and now, the system generally favoured is the Galilean, with a single lens in the foresight and, usually, a clearing lens in the backsight. At about the time of the change-over it became normal to put the wind scale on to the backsight. When standing to load at the muzzle it had been no great labour to set the wind at the same time and just before getting down to fire. Today the actual aiming element is probably usually a cross-hair but there are always those who stick to a ring, and others who prefer their own special arrangment. The telescope sight may look a better bet, and since the 1930s there has been a slowly growing percentage of firers using them, but it is possible to get completely confused over wind settings, and it is also easily deranged by an accidental blow.

10

The Shape of Things to Come

More than ever before we are seeing today a widening divergence between arms produced for leisure activities, and those intended for military purposes. On the one hand, there are military specifications for all weathers and all conditions and, above all, for intensive firepower. Whilst, on the other, there is a growing number of people prepared to spend increasing sums of money on excelling in their chosen sport or recreation. This is borne out by the differences between, say, the British Army's self-loading rifle and the Anschultz Super Match .22 LR target arm. Both are specialised pieces of design with few obvious similarities, yet they have quite a recent common ancestor in the bolt-action service rifle of the early twentieth century. Paradoxically, however, though they have changed so much in detailed appearance, small arms in general have fundamentally changed very little during this century.

The changes that are apparent are really those that one would expect. There is a marked move, for example, towards lightness and smaller size, towards the use of more durable materials such as stainless steels and alloys, and towards cheaper, more easily mass-produced components. When plating is used today, it flakes less readily, and plastics, though lacking the aesthetic attraction of wood, are less easily damaged and very much less easily broken than their predecessors.

The range of leisure arms is a wide one: it embraces arms peculiarly suited to a particular sport, as well as those which could be termed arms of convenience. There is nothing new about the concept of convenience arms, but what is novel is their present extent and continued growth. The walking-stick shotgun is a long-standing favourite – the ideal companion for an evening stroll where there are plenty of rabbits. Although it could be considered a concealed weapon, it is really one of convenience. At the opposite extreme the ultra-small pinfire revolvers sold as cuff-links or brooches are

Miniature arms have always attracted attention but few which function have been smaller than this pinfire revolver of current Austrian manufacture.

Walking stick shotguns. Typical examples in .410 *(above)* and 9mm W.S. calibre.

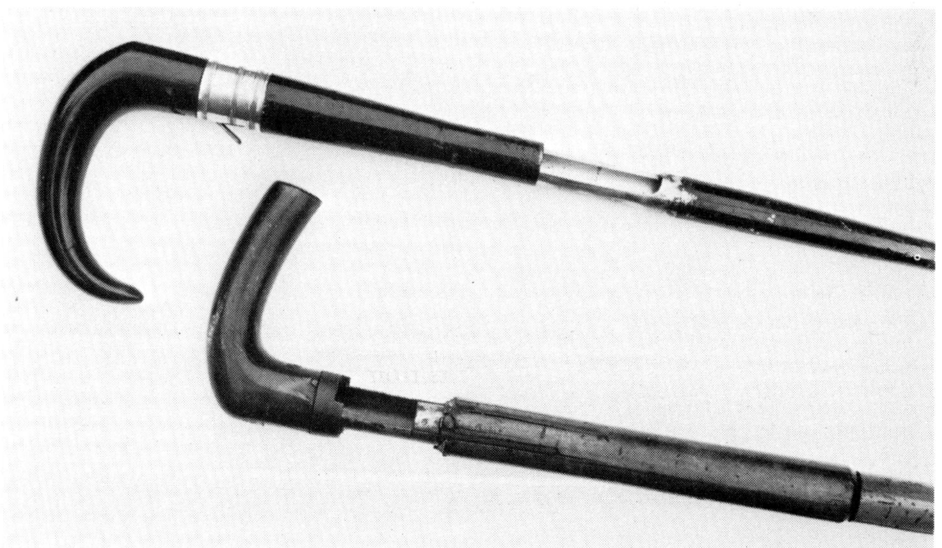

leisure arms which fulfil a decorative function within the broad scope of a leisure cult context. There is, of course, never anything new under the sun. The ultra-miniature Kolibri semi-automatic pistol made over fifty years ago was an equally desirable decorative possession for the man or woman who had everything!

If your shooting sport is plinking, as the Americans term it, picking off rabbits or small animals, then the time may come when the effort of carrying a full-length rifle may prove too much for you. It is more convenient to employ a pistol but it is also decidedly more difficult to hit your quarry. But now that someone has thought of sighting a pistol or revolver with a telescope sight, a new class of leisure sporting arms has been born which really has no earlier antecedent unless the rare nineteenth-century bull gun is admitted. In these arms the lock mechanism was buried in the stock actually behind the firer's eye as he used the weapon. In the modern telescope-sighted pistol the cartridge is in a slightly safer relationship to the eye, if, by any remote chance, a burst case or pierced primer releases a blast of gas.

Somewhat less dramatic are the modern convenience features which have appeared on some classes of arm. The best example is probably the 'dialable' choke. Instead of having to carry extra barrels or guns to deal with specialist applications of the shotgun such as wildfowling or game shooting, all the modern American sportsman has to do is set on the muzzle of his gun the choke setting appropriate to the distance he needs, remembering at the same time to use cartridges of appropriate load and shot size.

A by-product of the ceaseless quest for greater accuracy in leisure arms, if not for greater economy, has been the activity of hand-loading your own ammunition. This is now popular and can take the simple form of reloading, say, one revolver calibre by buying bullets from a dealer so that the minimum operation of decapping, recapping, measuring out the charge and seating the bullet is all that is required. At the opposite extreme, it can include casting and pressing the bullets, even with jackets, meticulously weighing charges and sizing the cases – as might be required perhaps for some forms of rifle shooting. It can be a matter of loading anywhere, on the corner of a convenient table, with a scissor-like multi-tool, or of operating on a special bench with a multi-station press and every modern refinement. Whatever time and effort the enthusiast wishes to devote to reloading he can usually see repaid in the accuracy of his shooting, not to mention the pleasure he derives from the creative process and the satisfaction from the economy of doing it himself. The only caution that must be sounded is that he is a free agent only within limits of bullet weight and size, charge weight and type, as laid down in guidance manuals to ensure the safety of the firer.

Hand-loading ammunition normally serves an orthodox form of target shooting, but in America there is a form of shooting entirely dedicated to the performance of different ammunition and barrel combinations. It is called bench rest shooting and is the unashamed pursuit of the ultimate in accuracy. As the name implies, the rifle is rested and the firer very comfortably positioned, usually seated, behind it. To help control flip and jump, the barrel and often also the stock are of a colossal size and weight.

The category of leisure arms also includes those arms which are not really for shooting at all. They may be fired but usually that is not the prime purpose in collecting modern commemorative arms. They are a form of investment. In the form of appropriate reissues of earlier celebrated models, companies like Colt chose to commemorate famous historical events. Just as some people have latent numismatic interests and cannot resist combining investing with a measure of collecting by purchasing special gold and silver commemorative medallions, so there are others who cannot resist owning a cabinet of Colt model 1911 .45 ACP semi-automatic pistols variously engraved to commemorate great American occasions, such as the Battle of Château Thierry in 1917.

The boundary is quite fine between arms which are commemorative medallions and those which are simply replicas of earlier famous models – such as the Peacemaker, the Winchester '66, or the Colt Navy revolver. It is probably more a matter of intention than anything else. There are many who desperately want to shoot such celebrated arms as the Pattern '53 rifle musket and who cannot afford to purchase an original in good condition. For them a replica may be an adequate substitute. It yields the experience of muzzle-loading and contending with the limitations of ammunition and rifle in trying to get a good score, even if it does not satisfy the romantic's desire for an intimate bridge in time – a sensation which many of us feel when firing a gun, knowing that perhaps a hundred years have lapsed since the last bullet travelled through the bore. Certainly the available British modern replicas of Enfield rifles and carbines are very good copies and they do permit competition shooting at the same time as safeguarding the survival in good order of the original arms. In consequence, very often muzzle-loading arms are shot in separate classes – originals and replicas.

The extent of public interest in such replica arms and the desire to own them should not be underestimated. In this country nowadays the value of replicas manufactured almost exceeds that of all the other leisure arms, if we exclude very fine and very expensive shotguns. The historian should welcome this trend, for not only does ownership of a good working replica often foster a genuine interest in the original and its invention and original use, but it also provides the modern enthusiast with an opportunity of making his mistakes as in care, in cleaning or transport, on a weapon where damage does not matter to the same degree.

Perhaps the most advanced developments in leisure arms occur in those designed for submarine use. Sea water is remarkably corrosive so the whole weapon has to be made of stainless steels, special alloys, bronzes and unbreakable plastics. To cope with different sizes of quarry encountered and to guard against damage to harpoons on rocks, a selection of blank powder cartridges of various strengths is available. These are colour-coded for rapid recognition.

At their most powerful, blank cartridge system underwater guns are much superior in performance to any rubber, spring or air-propelled gun. Whilst the usual target is a shark of adequate size, it is clear that such weapons could have military potential so there is a rather tenuous link with very specialist military arms. Another tenuous link is the missile itself which – in the case of underwater guns, a harpoon – can carry an explosive head. Not surprisingly, the same mixed feelings exist over their use as there were over using explosive bullets. Some people feel that there is a saving grace with the most recently developed form of head, which relies upon the sudden release of compressed gases in the large shark, as there is almost as much risk to the firer as to his quarry. If the head fails to penetrate sufficiently then the released gases act as a retrorocket and the harpoon is violently projected back at the firer!

'Survival' arms are also often very specialised in design and are as appropriate to the civilian airman forced down in the jungle, as they are to his military counterpart in a similar situation. In the Second World War an arm which could be considered to be in this category was the mass-produced, pressed-metal .45 ACP Liberator pistol. Today, however, a weapon like the Armalite take-down rifle would be considered a survival arm. In these the barrel and action are well protected inside the plastic butt until required. There is nothing new in the idea of using the butt as a container – the Mauser 1896 pistol did so – nor is it new to produce arms which readily dismantle. The novelty lies in combining the two, which is now possible with the wide range of non-corroding alloys and impervious plastics – not to mention efficient seals – on the market today.

In the military field proper the dominant development of the past hundred years has been the adoption of smaller and smaller calibres, resulting in lighter and lighter rounds. This means that if the soldier always carried the same weight of ammunition, he is now able to carry more cartridges, resulting in greater firepower. In early attempts to produce a high-powered, small-calibre cartridge, such as the .22 HP for the 1899 Savage, any saving in bullet weight was lost through the massive size of the case for the necessary propellant charge. In more modern small-calibre military rifles, as with the current 5.56mm family which is actually smaller than .22 ins, the entire cartridge is scaled down. This is made possible by modern powders. The soldier can therefore either benefit from a reduction in his overall burden or from an increase in his total firepower. It looks to be all gain, but there is one major drawback, a considerable loss in long-range accuracy.

A traditional limitation on the use of small arms has been the difficulty of aiming at the enemy by night. Here remarkable advances have been made in recent years. Rank, in their SS20 Mark 1 night sight, have almost given the soldier the ability to see and shoot in the dark without any extra light source. The SS20 sight magnifies by four times and intensifies the image up to 100,000 times. With this sight the British military sniper is probably better equipped for night fighting than any enemy: the fact that it costs about £2000 is not such a deterrent as it would be for a civilian customer.

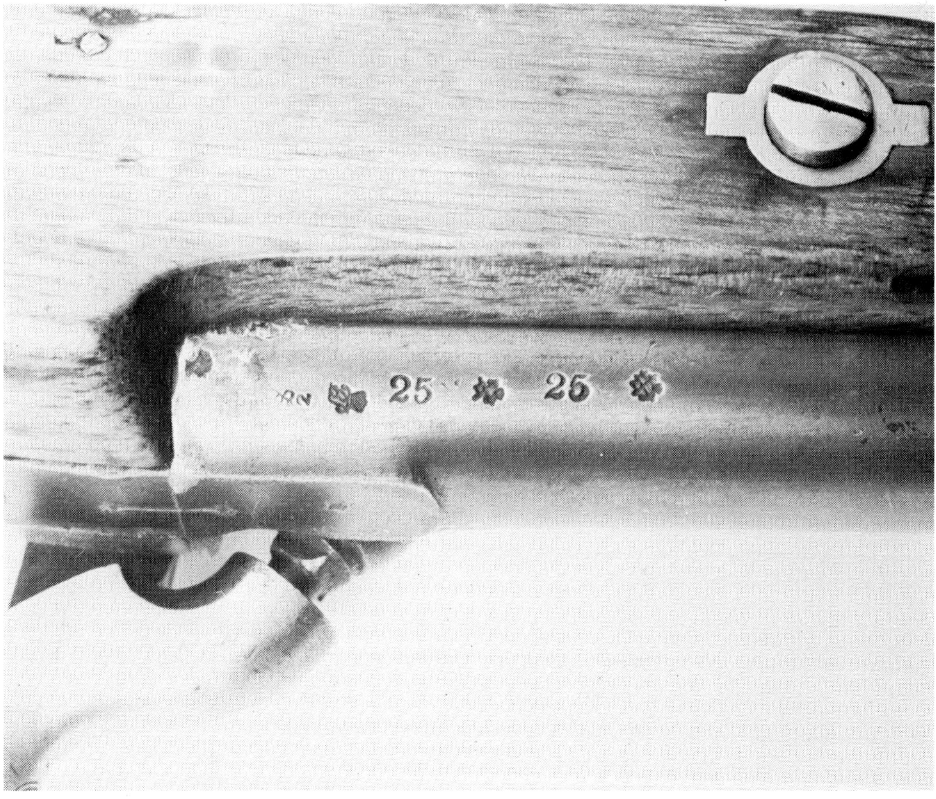

Proof and view marks invariably appear on British arms. This barrel has been inspected and punched at the Birmingham Proof House.

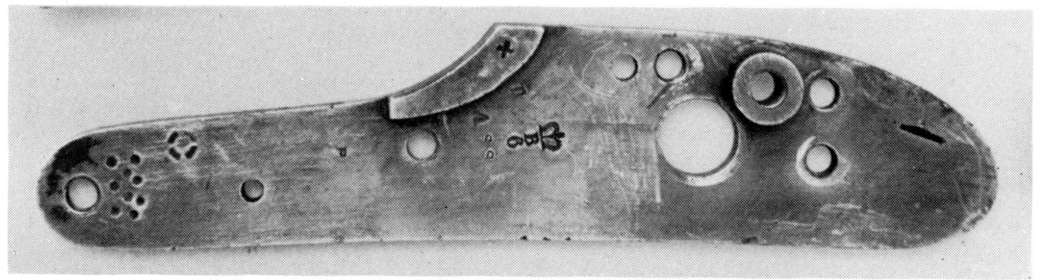

Every component on a military arm, as this lock plate, was inspected and punched appropriately. The crowned B is for Birmingham.

Military arms have also deviated from leisure arms in the materials from which they are made. The soldier is not concerned with the aesthetics of his weapon. The main desiderata are ease and cheapness of manufacture, durability, and simplicity of repair. Wood was bound to be an early casualty. Repairing wooden stocks by splicing is an expensive business – it is far cheaper to replace one black plastic injection moulding by another, that is if it ever breaks. The only real objection to plastic butts is the surface texture against the face in aiming and firing. Where pressings are inappropriate, then metal components made by investment-casting are almost invariably used. Very few components are now machined: usually only the breech block itself and some associated components are manufactured in this way.

Even the barrel is no longer made by a method which is linked to the traditional one. In the nineteenth century and the following decades a barrel was rifled by a machine which cut the rifling grooves individually. But for some years the military rifle barrel, and many target and match barrels, have been made by a process of hammering the barrel over a form of mandrel which is shaped to impart the required number, location and profile of grooves. The action of hammering the rifling also elongates the barrel to the required length.

The one thing that does not change in either military or leisure arms is quality control in manufacture. Everything is inspected during manufacture and after assembly. Barrels and actions are proofed – that is, fired with a specially powerful cartridge – and inspected to ensure that there is no resultant flaw or defect. Only if the components pass this inspection are they punched with the official proof marks. London, Birmingham and the Royal Small Arms Factory at Enfield each have their own proof marks.

Predicting the shape of the future is always hazardous. Perhaps it would not be too rash to suggest that the fully acceptable combustible cartridge may soon emerge. It was never competitive in the nineteenth century though in certain Westley Richards and Volcanic arms brave attempts were made. Soon advancing technology will offer perfect mechanical breech obturation and cartridge-case material which is genuinely totally consumed. But there is a catch. Although it may be a nuisance extracting and ejecting the fired case, in so doing much of the unwanted heat of firing is also removed: with consumable cartridges there would be a much increased risk of 'cook off', not to mention problems in use and storage arising in all weather and all temperatures.

The substitution of electrical or electronic, rather than mechanical, arrangements for firing the gun is another possibility. Although this is undoubtedly possible, there would probably be no advantage in durability over the conventional. The Russians tried it for Olympic shooting and the French have such an arm on sale. Unorthodox triggers are not new – thumb triggers are perhaps the most frequently encountered alternative, as in a formerly mass-produced Winchester .22 – but it is unlikely that electrical cartridge ignition will come for many decades. Apart from the size of the world's investment in conventional cartridge-manufacturing plants, there is the need for that very elusive, perfect lightweight battery.

What might the soldier of the 1980s be carrying? What kind of rifle? Where have the lines of development we have been tracing led to? The new rifle will have, so it seems, an option on automatic fire or single shots. It will be lightweight. It will suit any build from the small-framed Gurkha to the tallest European. No weight or space will be wasted when functional duplication can be achieved – so the magazine will sit behind the trigger and the whole configuration will be like a bull gun. A short-range use-limitation will avoid the need for a tall backsight and this in turn will make straight stocking fully practical, so clinching good fast shooting by instinctive pointing. It will make extensive use of stamping and plastics but will stick to traditional steels for real durability. In spite of its handy size the barrel will be long enough to keep good short-range accuracy, whilst its calibre, at 4.85 mm, will be small enough to ensure that the weight of the cartridge is as light as possible. Naturally with a basic design that is so rational, the gap between the rifle and the light-support weapon, the old light machine gun, will be narrowed closer still – for the latter will have just a slightly longer and heavier barrel, a larger magazine and an 80%-commonality of components. It will therefore be an excellent logistical solution.

This rifle, which could one day soon be the companion of the British soldier, will undoubtedly be the logical culmination of the design tendencies apparent within current military parameters. What it does is to emphasise more than ever the gulf between arms for leisure and arms for war. One reason for this is that the sub-optical sight, the short-range cartridge and calibre, the unconventional rearwards weighting of the balance, and the utilitarian appearance, fine though they may be in urban warfare and general military combat, represent the antithesis of the target and match rifleman's desiderata. *Chacun à son goût,* and each shall have the tool which serves him right!

Looking beyond the present configuration of guns, do we see the one-man, portable, battlefield surveillance radar of the present day developing, in miniaturised form, into an integral part of the rifle? Or do we see the Belgian jet-shot silent weapons system carving a real niche for itself in some more sophisticated form? A powerful, silent, flashless, smokeless system has much to recommend it. Or will the versatile laser in new guise become the ultimate in personal arms?

Whatever shape or shapes the future soldier's weapon takes there are those for whom the gun will always be an incomparable combination of finely engraved and beautifully blued steel, merging into polished and figured walnut.

Epilogue

Perhaps you have made your choice, perhaps you have not. Whether you decide upon an involvement in the field of arms or whether you choose to keep them at a distance: they are there. Never in history was it more true than if you want peace you should prepare for war. Let us hope that the present equilibrium between the two super powers, real or imagined – which perhaps makes little difference – continues. Whilst human nature remains as history has repeatedly shown it, peoples and nations will from time to time resort to force. We need go no further than Ireland for a reminder. But of course there is a difference between living in a society in peace preserved by the threat of war, and going out of one's way to enjoy the cultural and sporting heritage of arms.

The ten vignettes which have afforded us a look at the immense field of arms, or rather of the gun, have themselves constituted a severe constraint. They were chosen with care to reflect the major facets of the subject yet they have left so much unrevealed. There is, for example, little on the history of the semi-automatic pistol yet for many the only arms which really merit dedicated attention are the Luger and the Mauser. Perforce modern ordnance have been almost entirely left out of the account, also the machine gun, perhaps the greatest arbiter of man's destiny in this century, has been given very little space. The criterion has been simply what most closely affects or relates to the ordinary individual. So we have progressed from the weapon as a near essential element in individual survival, through the gun as a special embellishment, to the gun both as an instrument of leisure and a specialist tool in combat.

The great difficulty in the study of the gun is preserving objectivity. In many ways it is more problematical today than it was a hundred years ago. In any field of research there is no substitute for the study of the original sources one's self. Unfortunately there simply is not the time for more than a few of us to indulge in this and then in connection with only a very small amount of the total field. I had the good fortune to spend five years at Cambridge engaged in full-time research into the development of the rifle and its significance for contemporary society, between 1835 and 1870. Perhaps what impressed me most was the danger of depending upon contemporary authors for a true account of events. I had been brought up on such classics as W. W. Greener's *The Gun,* Colonel Peter Hawker's *Notes for Young Sportsmen,* and Deane's *Manual of Firearms,* not to mention Hans Busk's books on the Enfield rifle. Each of these was written by someone with an axe to grind, whether it was to sell more of his guns or to get more volunteers to rally to the flag, and as such the end justified the means. I doubt in fact whether much of the bias was conscious, it was simply inherent in the approach at the time. The lesson, however, is obvious – never rely upon a single secondary source. Go, whenever possible, to the arms and the records themselves.

Today the situation is both easier and more difficult. In the 1940s and 1950s to gain access to the major nineteenth-century secondary sources you had to have entry to a library of the standing of Cambridge University's. That has changed quite dramatically. In every direction, such has been the growing interest in the gun historically that there are publishers turning out facsimile editions of the classics. Indeed if you have the spare cash and only a little patience you can furnish yourself with a library of such volumes. Secondly, the situation is easier because the last twenty years has seen direct application to the field of firearms of relatively sophisticated techniques of historical research, developed over the past four or five decades in the universities. Perhaps, however, the most important improvement is that most of those who have been responsible for the new generation of secondary sources have been inspired by no other motive than bringing order and comprehension where previously chaos and confusion have reigned. Of course there is always the imponderable element of an author, who has not developed the necessary qualities in research falling short of his target; just as there is the less attractive possibility of a book being written on a previously unexplored sub-field simply to encourage others to collect in a difficult area with financial advantages accruing to the author who has previously ensured he has a ready stock! To be fair in the latter case, the quality of the research can still be very high and the final product a genuinely worthwhile contribution to scholarship.

So today the would-be collector or the would-be shooter is looked after both better and worse than his predecessors. The collector can find out more about his chosen sub-field than was possible ever before but *ipso facto* he has that much less opportunity of making his own original contribution to scholarship.

And, of course, he has that much less chance of picking up a bargain. The opportunities in shooting too have a somewhat similar complexion. Probably never before has the would-be shooter been better provided with clubs for .22 and air rifle practice, nor with arms and ammunition of greater absolute accuracy, yet he has largely lost the opportunity of attempting the really challenging forms of shooting which his predecessors enjoyed. Most people rate the virtual loss of the chance to shoot lions, tigers and elephants as a step in the right direction, being aware of the need for conservation, but few experienced marksmen would do other than jump at the chance of shooting at ultra long range.

With retrenchment policies dominant in the Ministry of Defence, and with the rapid run-down in our armed forces overseas, the last few years has seen a serious reduction in the number of military small arms ranges available in Britain. Unfortunately, coupled with the actual decline in the numbers of these ranges has come a marked increase in the military use of those that remain. As an undergraduate at Cambridge in the mid 1950s, I could and did go shooting on a long range three afternoons and more each week. Now at Cambridge my successors are fortunate to get one afternoon a fortnight. The situation has been worsened still further by the increasing specialisation of military shooting and the alteration of many ranges to electric target operation. Short range electric targets are small consolation for those who regard the acme of shooting in the traditional vein as being on a 10-foot target at 1200 yards or better still a 12-foot target at 1500 yards. The capital cost of a full-size long range is prohibitive these days so it is likely that we will remain beholden to the Ministry of Defence. Perhaps the only way to respond to the present situation is to hold on as determinedly as possible to every range allocation that comes our way.

When I write of the would-be collector and again of the would-be shooter I recognise the great dichotomy that exists and is likely to go on existing. It is simply the distinction between those whose interests centre mainly if not exclusively upon the arm itself, and those for whom the arm is purely a means to an end. What that end is, is difficult to determine. My best guess is that it is demonstrating or trying to demonstrate that your ability is greater than that of others. And according to the type of shooting, it ranges from an emphasis on wind judgement as in match rifle shooting, to an emphasis upon the steadiness of the hand as in pistol shooting. Unfortunately, there are not enough of us who are at once collectors, historians and marksmen to hold the two communities together. We try but the whole traditional development in the two great areas militates against success. In its petty form the dichotomy is perfectly epitomised in the marksman who acquires a fine example of the eight-inch-long barrelled Luger and, feeling that the backsight is less satisfactory for target shooting than one on a more modern pistol, has it ground off and another substituted. When the pistol is eventually worn out internally and placed on the market the collector weeps at the devastated sights. I have seen exactly this occur. The only hope seems to lie in the fact that even the most callous marksman may realise that the sum his vandalised pistol fetches is substantially less than the going rate for those less savagely treated.

In its more general form the dichotomy is far more serious. When marksmen speak for collector historians or the other way about injustice is likely. We live in a world always in a state of flux. After the 1937 Firearms Act came the 1968 Act and then the Green Paper. The Green Paper was a draft of proposals put forward by the police and the Home Office to limit the ownership of firearms still further. It should have been produced, if indeed it was required so soon after the 1968 Act, by a natural form of consultation between the police and Home Office, the shooting fraternity, perhaps as represented in the Long Room Committee, the historian collectors and the museums. In fact it was a document of amazingly narrow outlook almost entirely lacking a basis in consultation. Naturally it was opposed and very successfully too. Yet in all the campaign which was fought to achieve its amendments, there was little sign of a coming together of the two main fraternities. If proof were needed of the fundamental difference in outlook between those who study and collect and those who shoot guns, it was certainly furnished in 1972.

My purpose in describing the present division in the ranks of those for whom the gun is something special is to leave the reader in the position to make his own decisions intelligently. To me there is no division. A gun is part of our technological, military and social history; its possession today is both a tangible link with the past, a key to the good fellowship of those who enjoy it, whichever way that may be, and a means of deriving an immense amount of personal pleasure at no cost to other members of the community. Those sporting prints in reproduction which adorn so many of our drawing rooms remind us of the gun as part of the eighteenth-century rural scene, the pages of Dickens of its place in the nineteenth century, and the television news reports of the twentieth-century Olympics of the way that nations still compete with each other with the gun.

So make your decision, take your choice. Let others gently amuse you through television and books, let the challenge of the ranges inveigle you from your fireside chair, or let the fascination of the past lead you into the pleasures of ownership – joint ownership – of the gun.

Index

Numbers in italic refer to illustrations